Workbook

Apparel
Design, Textiles & Construction

Nancy Henke-Konopasek, CFCS
Munster, Indiana

Publisher
The Goodheart-Willcox Company, Inc.
Tinley Park, Illinois
www.g-w.com

Copyright © 2018
by
The Goodheart-Willcox Company, Inc.

All rights reserved. No part of this work may be reproduced, stored, or transmitted in any form or by any electronic or mechanical means, including information storage and retrieval systems, without the prior written permission of The Goodheart-Willcox Company, Inc.

Manufactured in the United States of America.

ISBN: 978-1-63126-562-4

1 2 3 4 5 6 7 8 9 – 18 – 22 21 20 19 18 17 16

The Goodheart-Willcox Company, Inc. Brand Disclaimer: Brand names, company names, and illustrations for products and services included in this text are provided for educational purposes only and do not represent or imply endorsement or recommendation by the author or the publisher.

The Goodheart-Willcox Company, Inc. Safety Notice: The reader is expressly advised to carefully read, understand, and apply all safety precautions and warnings described in this book or that might also be indicated in undertaking the activities and exercises described herein to minimize risk of personal injury or injury to others. Common sense and good judgment should also be exercised and applied to help avoid all potential hazards. The reader should always refer to the appropriate manufacturer's technical information, directions, and recommendations; then proceed with care to follow specific equipment operating instructions. The reader should understand these notices and cautions are not exhaustive.

The publisher makes no warranty or representation whatsoever, either expressed or implied, including but not limited to equipment, procedures, and applications described or referred to herein, their quality, performance, merchantability, or fitness for a particular purpose. The publisher assumes no responsibility for any changes, errors, or omissions in this book. The publisher specifically disclaims any liability whatsoever, including any direct, indirect, incidental, consequential, special, or exemplary damages resulting, in whole or in part, from the reader's use or reliance upon the information, instructions, procedures, warnings, cautions, applications, or other matter contained in this book. The publisher assumes no responsibility for the activities of the reader.

The Goodheart-Willcox Company, Inc. Internet Disclaimer: The Internet resources and listings in this Goodheart-Willcox Publisher product are provided solely as a convenience to you. These resources and listings were reviewed at the time of publication to provide you with accurate, safe, and appropriate information. Goodheart-Willcox Publisher has no control over the referenced websites and, due to the dynamic nature of the Internet, is not responsible or liable for the content, products, or performance of links to other websites or resources. Goodheart-Willcox Publisher makes no representation, either expressed or implied, regarding the content of these websites, and such references do not constitute an endorsement or recommendation of the information or content presented. It is your responsibility to take all protective measures to guard against inappropriate content, viruses, or other destructive elements.

Cover image: Left to right, top to bottom: Diego Cervo/Shutterstock.com, Kzenon/Shutterstock.com, michaeljung/Shutterstock.com, wavebreakmedia/Shutterstock.com, ©iStock.com/Wavebreakmedia

Contents

Part 1 Apparel and Fashion

Chapter 1
Understanding Clothing..........7
  A. Why People Wear Clothes 7
  B. Personality, Values, and
     Self-Concept 12
  C. First Impressions 13
  D. Clothing Choices 14

Chapter 2
Understanding Fashion..........15
  A. Styles, Fashions, Classics,
     and Fads 15
  B. Fashion Cycles 19
  C. Neckline and Collar Identification ..21
  D. Sleeve, Blouse, and Shirt Styles 23
  E. Skirt and Pant Styles 24
  F. Dress Style Identification 25
  G. Jacket and Coat Style Match-Up 26

Chapter 3
Textiles and Apparel
Through the Years 27
  A. Cultural Influences on Fashion 27
  B. Apparel Time Line—Stone Age
     to Space Age 29
  C. Historical Influences on Apparel....30

Chapter 4
The Textile and Apparel Industry ..31
  A. Textiles in the Future 31
  B. The Textile and Apparel Industry ...32
  C. Textile and Apparel Careers Match..35
  D. Vertical Integration...............36

Chapter 5
The Worldwide Apparel Industry ..37
  A. Made in the USA 37
  B. Safe Work Environment
     Responsibilities.................38
  C. Computers in Textiles and
     Apparel 39
  D. Worldwide Apparel Industry
     Review 40

Chapter 6
A Closer Look at
Fashion Design...................41
  A. You, the Designer 41
  B. Featured Fashion Designer........42
  C. Communicating Fashion News 43
  D. Exploring a Trade Association 44

Part 2 Apparel Decisions

Chapter 7
Planning a Wardrobe..............45
  A. Wardrobe Inventory..............45
  B. Clothing Wants..................46
  C. Mixing and Matching.............47
  D. Accessory Wardrobe 48
  E. Selecting Appropriate Clothes 49

Chapter 8
Apparel Decisions and Choices ...53
  A. Using the Decision-Making
     Process.........................53
  B. Factors Affecting Family Clothing
     Decisions........................54
  C. Wardrobe Additions 55
  D. To Sew or to Buy.................56

Chapter 9
Consumer Rights and
Responsibilities 57
  A. Using Labels 57
  B. Generic Names and
     Trademark Names 58
  C. Labeling Legislation 59
  D. Labeling.........................60
  E. Consumer Complaint 61

Chapter 10
Choices as a Consumer 63
- A. Where to Shop for Clothes 63
- B. Shopping Strategies 65
- C. Advertising 67
- D. Consumer Shopping Terms 68

Chapter 11
Get Your Money's Worth 69
- A. Quality Counts 69
- B. Inspecting for Quality 71
- C. Making the Most of Accessories 73
- D. My Preferences 74

Chapter 12
Selecting Apparel for Family Members 75
- A. Choosing Clothes for Family Members 75
- B. Selecting Clothes for Children 79
- C. Clothes for People with Physical Disabilities 80

Chapter 13
Keeping Apparel Looking Its Best 81
- A. Clothing Care Do's and Don'ts 81
- B. Stain Removal 82
- C. Comparing Laundry Products 84

Chapter 14
Laundry and Dry Cleaning 85
- A. Caring for Clothes 85
- B. Choose the Right Temperature 87
- C. Professional Dry Cleaning 88

Chapter 15
Repair, Redesign, and Recycle 89
- A. Keeping Your Clothes Wearable ... 89
- B. Altering for a Better Fit 90
- C. Clothing Repair and Alterations ... 91
- D. Redesigning and Recycling Ideas ... 92

Part 3 Color and Design

Chapter 16
Color 93
- A. Reactions to Color 93
- B. Color Basics 95
- C. Color Schemes and Combinations ... 97
- D. Color and Your Clothes 99
- E. Color Trends 100

Chapter 17
The Elements and Principles of Design 101
- A. Basic Figure/Physique Types 101
- B. Using the Elements of Design 102
- C. Creating Illusions with Lines 103
- D. Using the Principles of Design 104

Part 4 From Fibers to Fabrics

Chapter 18
The Natural Fibers 107
- A. Fiber Fill-in-the-Blanks 107
- B. Natural Fiber Facts 108
- C. Natural Fibers and Prices 109
- D. Natural Fiber Research 110

Chapter 19
The Manufactured Fibers 111
- A. Manufactured Fiber Facts 111
- B. Manufactured Fibers and Prices ... 113
- C. Manufactured Fiber Research 114

Chapter 20
From Yarn to Fabric 115
- A. Yarn and Fabric Term Review 115
- B. Single, Ply, and Chord Yarns 117
- C. Woven and Knitted Fabrics 118
- D. Fabric Construction 119

Chapter 21
Fabric Color and Finishes 121
- A. Textile Color and Finishes Technology 121
- B. Adding Color to Textiles 122

  C. Dyeing and Printing 123
  D. Finishes 124

Part 5 Sewing Techniques

Chapter 22
Figure Types and Pattern Sizes . . . 125
  A. Figure Types 125
  B. Patterns and Measuring Techniques. 126
  C. Your Measurements 127
  D. Selecting a Pattern 128

Chapter 23
Selecting Patterns and Fabrics 129
  A. Patterns and Projects 129
  B. Reading a Pattern Envelope 130
  C. Pattern Symbols 131
  D. Choosing the Right Pattern Designs 132

Chapter 24
Sewing Equipment 133
  A. Equipment Uses 133
  B. Notions 135
  C. Sewing Machine—Part Identification. 136
  D. Sewing Machine Problem Detective .138

Chapter 25
Getting Ready to Sew 139
  A. Fabric Grain 139
  B. Altering the Pattern 140
  C. Cutting Layouts 141
  D. Pinning the Pattern Pieces 142

Chapter 26
Basic Sewing Skills 143
  A. Directional Sewing 143
  B. Seams and Seam Finishes 144
  C. Facings and Interfacings 146
  D. Hem Finishes and Hems 147

Chapter 27
Advanced Sewing Skills. 149
  A. Collars 149
  B. Sleeves 150
  C. Pockets. 151
  D. Sewing with Knits and Pile Fabrics 152

Chapter 28
Serging Skills 153
  A. Sergers 153
  B. Serger Machine Parts. 154
  C. Serger Stitch Identification 156
  D. Parts of Serger Stitches 157
  E. Serger Problems and Solutions 158

Part 6 Career Preparation

Chapter 29
Preparing for a Career 159
  A. Leadership Skills and Traits 159
  B. Effective Working Relationships . . .160
  C. Student Organizations. 161
  D. Parliamentary Procedure and Meetings .162

Chapter 30
A Job and a Career 163
  A. A Career in Textiles and Apparel. . .163
  B. Self-Study .164
  C. Preparing a Résumé. 165
  D. A Cover Message 166
  E. Filling out a Job Application Form. 167
  F. The Job Interview. 169
  G. Using Time Wisely 170

Chapter 31
Entrepreneurship—Profiting from Your Skills 171
  A. Entrepreneur Interview. 171
  B. Profiting from Your Skills 173
  C. Entrepreneurship 174

Introduction

This workbook is designed for use with the text, *Apparel: Design, Textiles & Construction*. As you complete these activities, you can review the facts and concepts the text provides. You will be able to apply these facts and concepts as you select, buy, and care for your apparel. Textile activities help you to understand fabrics, while sewing construction activities help you learn new sewing skills. You will also be able to investigate careers in textiles and apparel and learn how to prepare for them.

The best way to use this workbook is to begin by reading your assignment in the text. You will find that the activities in the workbook correspond to the chapters in *Apparel: Design, Textiles & Construction*. Follow the directions carefully at the beginning of each activity. You will find a variety of the activities, such as fill-in-the-blanks, that can be used as study guides to review for tests and quizzes. Do your best to complete these activities carefully and accurately. Other activities will help you apply what you have learned by using design skills, making comparisons, using sewing skills, and expressing your opinions.

The activities in this workbook have been designed to be both interesting and fun to do. These activities will allow you to express your creativity and develop skills related to apparel design, selection, and basic apparel construction techniques. The more thought and effort you put into these activities, the more you will learn from them.

Chapter 1

Understanding Clothing

Why People Wear Clothes

Activity A Name _____

Chapter 1 Date _____ Period _____

The five basic types of needs cited by Abraham Maslow are identified above each of the boxes in this activity. Look through magazines, catalogs, or online sources to find pictures of people wearing clothes to meet these needs. Paste a copy of the image or the URL address in the space provided. Then, describe how the clothing meets the human need.

Physical need: _____
_____

(Continued)

Activity A, continued   Name _____

Safety and security need: _____
_____

Activity A, continued   Name_____

Love and acceptance need:_____
_____

(Continued)

Chapter 1   Understanding Clothing

Activity A, continued Name _____

Esteem need: _____
_____

(Continued)

Activity A, continued   Name_____

Self-actualization need: _____
_____

Chapter 1   Understanding Clothing

Personality, Values, and Self-Concept

Activity B Name _____

Chapter 1 Date _____ Period _____

Look through magazines, catalogs, or online sources to find a photo of an outfit that you believe reflects your personality, values, and self-concept. Paste a copy of the image or the URL address in the space provided. Then, respond to the statements that follow.

[   ]

This outfit reflects the following aspects of my personality: _____
_____
_____

This outfit reflects the following values I consider important or desirable: _____
_____
_____

If I wore this outfit, my self-concept would be: _____
_____

First Impressions

Activity C   **Name** _____

Chapter 1   **Date** _____   **Period** _____

Find four pictures of people from online sources or magazines and paste a copy of the images or the URL addresses in the spaces provided. For each image, describe your first impressions of each person's appearance. Share your impressions with the class.

Chapter 1   Understanding Clothing   13

Clothing Choices

Activity D Name _____

Chapter 1 Date _____ Period _____

Many factors affect clothing choices. Respond to the following statements and questions about your own clothing choices.

1. List your activities. _____
   _____
   _____

2. How do your activities influence your apparel choices? _____
   _____
   _____

3. Describe the climate in your area. (Also describe the climate in any area you may visit.) _____
   _____
   _____
   _____

4. How does climate affect your clothing choices? _____
   _____
   _____

5. Describe apparel that you feel (or that others have told you) looks most flattering on you. _____
   _____
   _____
   _____

6. In what ways do family members or friends influence your apparel choices? _____
   _____
   _____
   _____

7. How does the cost of clothes affect your clothing choices? _____
   _____
   _____

8. How does the media influence your apparel choices? _____
   _____
   _____

Chapter 2
Understanding Fashion

Styles, Fashions, Classics, and Fads

Activity A   **Name** _____

Chapter 2   **Date** _____ **Period** _____

Look through magazines, catalogs, or online sources to find photos that illustrate the differences among styles, fashions, classics, and fads. Paste a copy of the images or the URL addresses under the appropriate headings. Then, explain why each is a style, fashion, classic, or fad. As an alternative, use a school-approved Web-based application to create a blog or webpage to illustrate your choices. Collaborate with your peers about whether each is a style, fashion, classic, or fad.

Examples of styles:

Definition of a style: _____

_____

(Continued)

Activity A, continued Name_____

Examples of fashions:

Definition of a fashion: _____
_____

(Continued)

Activity A, continued   Name_____

Examples of classics:

Definition of a classic:_____

_____

(Continued)

Activity A, continued   Name _____

Examples of fads:

```
┌─────────────────────────────────────────────────────────────┐
│                                                             │
│                                                             │
│                                                             │
│                                                             │
│                                                             │
│                                                             │
│                                                             │
│                                                             │
│                                                             │
│                                                             │
└─────────────────────────────────────────────────────────────┘
```

Definition of a fad: _____

_____

Fashion Cycles

Activity B   **Name** _____

Chapter 2   **Date** _____ **Period** _____

Interview older adults to find out about what fashions were like during the decades that follow. Record their comments in the space provided. Analyze your interview results. On the following page, write a report noting which fashions have cycled and how historical, economic, social, and cultural events influenced these cycles.

1940s: _____
_____
_____

1950s: _____
_____
_____

1960s: _____
_____
_____

1970s: _____
_____
_____
_____

1980s: _____
_____
_____
_____

1990s: _____
_____
_____

2000s: _____
_____
_____

(Continued)

Activity B, continued   Name_____

Fashion cycles survey analysis report: _____

Neckline and Collar Identification

Activity C   Name _____

Chapter 2   Date _____   Period _____

Identify the neckline and collar illustrations that follow. Write your answers in the space provided.

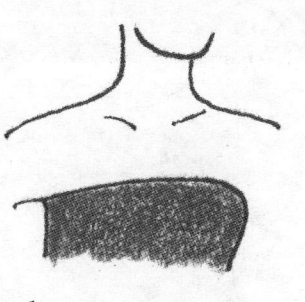  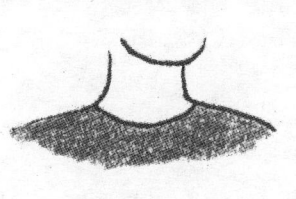 

1. _____ 2. _____ 3. _____ 4. _____

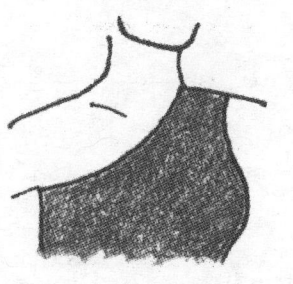 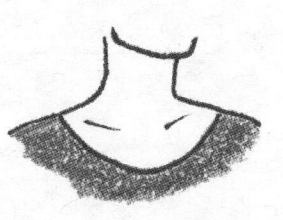 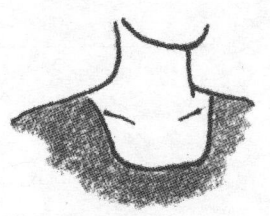 

5. _____ 6. _____ 7. _____ 8. _____

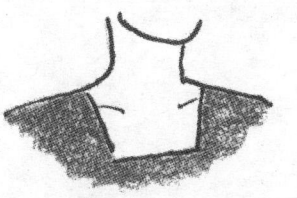  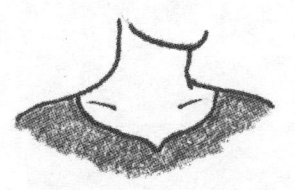 

9. _____ 10. _____ 11. _____ 12. _____

  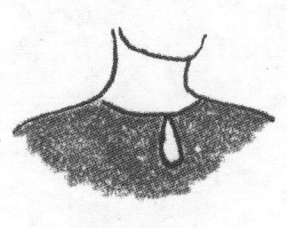 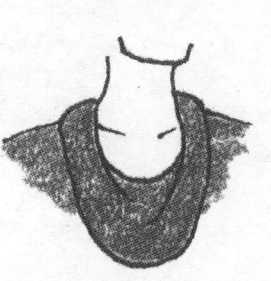

13. _____ 14. _____ 15. _____ 16. _____

(Continued)

Chapter 2   Understanding Fashion

Activity C, continued   Name_____

 17. _____

 18. _____

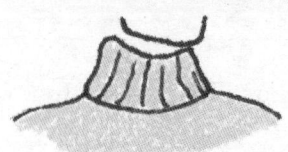 19. _____

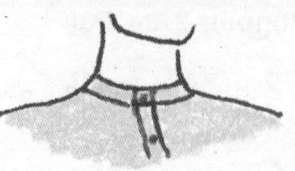 20. _____

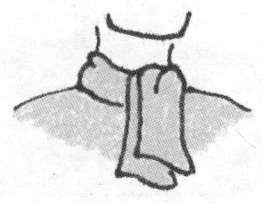 21. _____

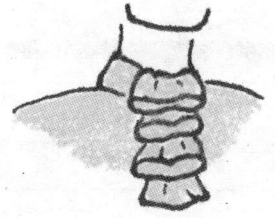 22. _____

 23. _____

 24. _____

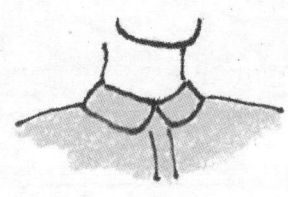 25. _____

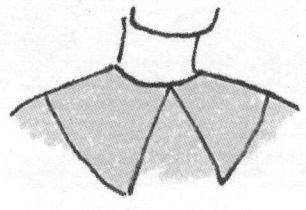 26. _____

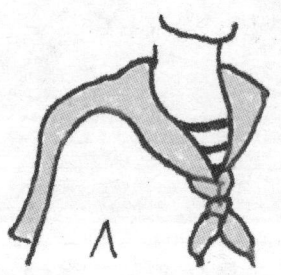 27. _____

 28. _____

 29. _____

 30. _____

Sleeve, Blouse, and Shirt Styles

Activity D Name _____

Chapter 2 Date _____ Period _____

Match the items in the right column to their correct definitions in the left column. Write your answer in the space provided. (*Note:* Some items may have more than one correct answer. Some answers may not be used.)

_____ 1. Sleeve that is attached to the body of the garment with a seam that circles the armhole near the shoulder.

_____ 2. Sleeve that is an extension of the garment front and back.

_____ 3. Sleeve that features diagonal seams in the front and back that extend from the neck to under the arms.

_____ 4. A variation of the set-in sleeve.

_____ 5. A variation of the kimono sleeve.

_____ 6. Sleeve that may be set in or an extension of the shoulder

_____ 7. A short, close-fitting, sleeveless top usually made of knit fabric.

_____ 8. A woman's sleeveless sweater or blouse, often worn under a jacket.

_____ 9. A blouse that covers the body from the bust to the waist with thin shoulder straps.

_____ 10. A more casual version of a man's dress shirt.

_____ 11. A blouse that was introduced in the early nineteenth century as an item of underwear worn between the corset and dress.

_____ 12. A tailored upper garment, similar to men's shirts.

_____ 13. A shirt featuring a stitched-pleat front that is bib-like in shape.

_____ 14. A blouse that features full, puffed-sleeves created by elastic or drawstrings at the neck and sleeve edges.

A. batwing
B. bell
C. bib front
D. bishop
E. butterfly
F. camisole
G. cap
H. cap with seam
I. cape
J. dolman
K. fitted
L. Juliet
M. kimono
N. leg-of-mutton
O. peasant
P. petal
Q. raglan
R. roll-up
S. set-in
T. shell
U. sport shirt
V. tank top
W. trumpet
X. western

Skirt and Pant Styles

Activity E Name _____

Chapter 2 Date _____ Period _____

In the space provided, write the name of the skirt or pant style described for each number that follows.

_____ 1. This skirt is the slimmest and falls straight from the hipline.

_____ 2. A type of trouser in which the legs are the same width from the knee to the hem with a 15-inch leg opening.

_____ 3. This style flares slightly from the hipline to the hemline, forming an "A" shape.

_____ 4. A type of skirt that is fitted at the waistline and flares out at the hem.

_____ 5. A skirt with regular sharp folds of fabric evenly spaced around the waist.

_____ 6. A type of pleat made of two fabric folds turned inward toward each other.

_____ 7. This skirt has gathers at the waistline before falling straight to the hem.

_____ 8. A skirt that is much fuller at the hemline.

_____ 9. A skirt that is full at the hemline.

_____ 10. When opened and laid flat, this style skirt forms a circle.

_____ 11. A variation of the wrap skirt that is knotted at the side.

_____ 12. A style of pants in which the legs are narrower at the hem than at the knee with a 13-inch leg opening.

_____ 13. The legs of these pants are tight-fitting through the thigh but flare out at the knee, forming a bell shape.

_____ 14. The legs are wider at the hem than at the knee and can begin above the knee, closer to the waist.

_____ 15. Pants that are full at the waist and flare widely at the hem.

_____ 16. A classic garment made of denim fabric with double stitching, and typically five pockets.

_____ 17. The waistline of these jeans or pants sits on the upper hips, below the natural waistline.

_____ 18. The legs gather into a band just below the knee.

_____ 19. Pants with wide legs that give the appearance of a skirt.

_____ 20. Also known as *warm-ups* or *sweat pants*, this garment is usually made of knit fabrics that are elasticized at the waist and ankle.

Dress Style Identification

Activity F   Name _____

Chapter 2   Date _____   Period _____

Identify the dress styles illustrated below. Write your answers in the space provided.

1. _____   2. _____   3. _____   4. _____

5. _____   6. _____   7. _____   8. _____

9. _____   10. _____   11. _____   12. _____

Chapter 2   Understanding Fashion

Copyright Goodheart-Willcox Co., Inc. May not be reproduced or posted to a publicly accessible website.

Jacket and Coat Style Match-Up

Activity G   Name _____

Chapter 2   Date _____   Period _____

Match the jacket and coat styles in the right column with the appropriate description in the left column. Write the letter of the correct answer in the space provided. (*Note:* Some answers may not be used.) Then use a school-approved Web application to create your own blog about jacket and coat styles. Locate image examples on the Web (citing the source) to use with your blog page. Collaborate with your classmates about your selections. Do they accurately represent the style?

_____ 1. An open, sleeveless or sleeved jacket that reaches almost to the waist.

_____ 2. A short, collarless jacket featuring braid trim and patch pockets.

_____ 3. A short jacket tightly gathered at the waist and cuffs.

_____ 4. A garment has a single row of buttons up the front.

_____ 5. A garment has two rows of buttons and the sides have a wider overlap.

_____ 6. A heavy, double-breasted, hip-length jacket originally worn by sailors.

_____ 7. A belted, hip-length jacket featuring patch pockets with button flaps.

_____ 8. A collarless jacket or sweater that opens down the front.

_____ 9. A hooded coat made with a quilt technique.

_____ 10. A garment with three cut-outs for the arms and head.

_____ 11. A loose, belted, double-breasted raincoat that features a double yoke across the shoulders.

_____ 12. A sleeveless outer garment that fits closely at the neck and hangs loosely over the shoulders.

_____ 13. A camel-colored wool coat with a full skirt at the back.

_____ 14. Coat that features long lines and a black velvet collar.

A. aviator/bomber
B. bolero
C. cape
D. cardigan
E. Chanel
F. chesterfield
G. coachman
H. double-breasted
I. pea jacket
J. polo
K. poncho
L. quilted parka
M. safari
N. single-breasted
O. trench coat
P. wrap

Chapter 3: Textiles and Apparel Through the Years

Cultural Influences on Fashion

Activity A Name _____

Chapter 3 Date _____ Period _____

Interview a foreign exchange student or someone else from another country. Find out the answers to the following questions. Write your answers in the space provided.

1. How do fashions in your country differ from those in the United States? _____
   _____
   _____
   _____

2. Have you seen any influences from your country reflected in fashions in the United States? If so, describe. _____
   _____
   _____
   _____

3. Describe any traditional garments or costumes people wear in your country. _____
   _____
   _____
   _____

4. What factors most influence fashions in your country? _____
   _____
   _____
   _____

5. Describe a typical teen's wardrobe in your country. _____
   _____
   _____
   _____

(Continued)

Activity A, continued   Name_____

6. Do fashions change quickly in your country? Why or why not?_____
   _____
   _____

7. Are fad fashions popular in your country? If so, describe some examples. _____
   _____
   _____

8. Describe how each of the following influences affect what people wear in your country. Give an example of each.

   Cultural influences:_____
   _____
   _____
   _____

   Social influences: _____
   _____
   _____
   _____

   Religious influences:_____
   _____
   _____
   _____

   Political influences: _____
   _____
   _____
   _____

   Economic influences: _____
   _____
   _____
   _____

   Technological influences: _____
   _____
   _____
   _____

Apparel Time Line—Stone Age to Space Age

Activity B   Name _____

Chapter 3   Date _____ Period _____

Create a time line illustrating significant events in textile and apparel history in the space provided. Compare and discuss your time line to those of others in the class.

Stone Age

_____
_____
_____
_____
_____
_____
_____
_____
_____
_____
_____
_____
_____
_____
_____
_____
_____
_____
_____
_____
_____
_____
_____
_____
_____

Space Age

Historical Influences on Apparel

Activity C   Name _____

Chapter 3   Date _____ Period _____

Complete the following exercises related to historical influences on fashion. Write your responses in the space provided.

1. Name three historical influences on apparel. Give an example of how each has influenced apparel. _____
_____
_____
_____
_____
_____
_____
_____

2. Match the clothing styles that follow with the times during which they were popular. Write the letter of the correct response in the space provided.

    _____ 1. 1700s

    _____ 2. 1800s

    _____ 3. 1920s

    _____ 4. 1940s

    _____ 5. 1950s

    _____ 6. 1970s

A   B

C   D   E   F

Apparel: Design, Textiles & Construction Workbook

Chapter 4: The Textile and Apparel Industry

Textiles in the Future

Activity A   **Name** _____

Chapter 4   **Date** _____ **Period** _____

Imagine it is 100 years from now. Make predictions about various types and uses of textiles in the following areas. Discuss your predictions in class.

Clothing uses: _____
_____
_____

Household uses: _____
_____
_____

Medical uses: _____
_____
_____

Industrial uses: _____
_____
_____

Space exploration: _____
_____
_____

Other predictions: _____
_____
_____
_____
_____

Copyright Goodheart-Willcox Co., Inc. May not be reproduced or posted to a publicly accessible website.

The Textile and Apparel Industry

Activity B   **Name** _____

Chapter 4   **Date** _____   **Period** _____

Manufacturing textiles and apparel requires many skilled people to get the job done. Next to each of the following occupations, briefly describe the role individuals in each position probably had in producing and merchandising the garment you are now wearing.

Describe the garment you are now wearing: _____

_____

_____

_____

1. Textile designer: _____

_____

_____

2. Textile converter: _____

_____

_____

3. Textile manufacturer: _____

_____

_____

4. Textile engineer: _____

_____

_____

5. Laboratory technician: _____

_____

_____

(Continued)

Activity B, continued   Name_____

6. Market analyst: _____
_____
_____
_____
_____

7. Fashion designer: _____
_____
_____
_____
_____

8. Sewing machine operator: _____
_____
_____
_____
_____

9. Finisher: _____
_____
_____
_____
_____

10. Quality control engineer: _____
_____
_____
_____
_____

11. Merchandise manager: _____
_____
_____
_____
_____

12. Buyer: _____
_____
_____
_____
_____

13. Sales associate: _____
_____
_____
_____
_____

(Continued)

Activity B, continued Name _____

14. Stock clerk: _____
_____
_____
_____

15. Market researcher: _____
_____
_____
_____

16. Fashion coordinator: _____
_____
_____
_____

17. Display director: _____
_____
_____
_____

18. Fashion illustrator: _____
_____
_____
_____

19. Fashion writer: _____
_____
_____
_____

20. Fashion model: _____
_____
_____
_____

21. Alterations specialist: _____
_____
_____
_____

Textile and Apparel Careers Match

Activity C Name _____

Chapter 4 Date _____ Period _____

Match the following textile and apparel careers with their descriptions. Write the letter of the correct response in the space provided.

_____ 1. Develops designs for fabrics, color combinations, patterns, prints, and weaves.

_____ 2. Decides what fibers to use, what widths and weights of fabrics to weave or knit, and how many yards to produce.

_____ 3. Performs tests on fibers, yarns, and fabrics in a laboratory.

_____ 4. Studies fashion changes and consumer demands.

_____ 5. Creates the designs and ideas for new clothes and accessories.

_____ 6. Sews a new design together.

_____ 7. Decides how to place the pattern pieces to prevent as much fabric waste as possible.

_____ 8. Sews the pieces together, generally in assembly-line fashion.

_____ 9. Sews the final details on garments, adding outside stitching or any hand sewing the garments require.

_____ 10. Removes loose threads, lint, and spots from the finished products.

_____ 11. Supervises all aspects of production activities in the plant.

_____ 12. Determines the price of producing an item of clothing or an accessory.

_____ 13. Develops standards of quality for garments and meeting those standards.

_____ 14. Responsible for the operation of one or more departments within a store; plans seasonal sales, promotional sales, and special events; and decides what merchandise to sell and at what price.

_____ 15. Responsible for selecting the clothes and accessories to sell in the stores.

_____ 16. Keeps merchandise displays attractive, receives payments and packages the items sold, and may be responsible for handling exchanges and returns.

_____ 17. Receives merchandise from delivery trucks, comparing delivery tickets with merchandise received, and prepares price tags.

_____ 18. Studies what customers want and need, finding out what is selling and what customers would buy if available on the market.

_____ 19. Works with the advertising and publicity departments for stores, to correlate advertising, promotional, and merchandising efforts.

_____ 20. Creates the attractive displays seen in store windows.

_____ 21. Works for retail stores, pattern companies, and advertising agencies, showing construction details, fabric textures, fabric designs, and fashionable accessories.

_____ 22. Through regular columns or articles, shows and explains new fashions to readers.

_____ 23. Appears in photos for press releases, Internet and mail-order catalogs, pattern catalogs, advertisements, and fashion shows.

_____ 24. Sews well, works fast, and decides what fitting problems exist and resolves them.

A. Alterations specialist
B. Buyer
C. Costing engineer
D. Display director
E. Fashion coordinator
F. Fashion designer
G. Fashion illustrator
H. Fashion model
I. Fashion writer
J. Finisher
K. Laboratory technician
L. Marker
M. Market analyst
N. Market researcher
O. Merchandise manager
P. Production manager
Q. Quality control engineer
R. Sales associate
S. Sample maker
T. Sewing machine operator
U. Stock clerk
V. Textile converter
W. Textile designer
X. Trimmer

Vertical Integration

Activity D   **Name** _____

Chapter 4   **Date** _____ **Period** _____

In the space provided, define *vertical integration*. Then use online sources or current trade journals to choose a textile or apparel company to research. Answer the questions that follow about this company in the space provided.

Vertical integration: _____

_____

_____

Company: _____

What does the company produce? _____

_____

_____

What operations does this company perform? _____

_____

_____

What steps does this company perform in creating its products? _____

_____

_____

_____

_____

_____

Do the operations take place at different plant locations? _____ If so, where? _____

_____

Explain how you think vertical integration might affect this company's cost control.

_____

_____

_____

_____

_____

_____

Chapter 5: The Worldwide Apparel Industry

Made in the USA

Activity A   Name _____

Chapter 5   Date _____ Period _____

Presume you are a candidate running for congress and you are at a press conference. Respond to the following questions in the space provided.

1. What does the label *Made in the USA* mean to you? _____
   _____

2. What effect do you feel the apparel industry has on the U.S. balance of trade? _____
   _____

3. Since U.S. apparel manufacturers must comply with government safety regulations and provide higher wages and benefits to employees, how can they compete with other countries that can mass-produce garments at a lower cost? _____
   _____

4. How does the trade deficit—created by the U.S. importing millions of dollars in textiles and apparel products each year—impact world economies? _____
   _____

5. What effect do you believe Free Trade Agreements (FTA) have on the U.S. economy? _____
   _____

6. How would you eliminate illegal sweatshops in this country as well as in other countries? _____
   _____

7. What effect do you believe the Fair Labor Standards Act had on the apparel industry? _____
   _____

8. What role do you feel the Occupational Safety and Health Administration plays in the apparel industry? _____
   _____

9. What do you believe is the economic effect of U.S. companies taking advantage of the low-cost labor supply outside the United Sates? _____
   _____

Safe Work Environment Responsibilities

Activity B   Name _____

Chapter 5   Date _____ Period _____

In the space below, define OSHA. Then think about the responsibilities both employees and employers share for a safe work environment. Responsibilities are listed below. If the responsibility is an employee responsibility, write *employee* in the blank. If the responsibility is an employer responsibility, write *employer* in the blank. Then respond to the question that follows at the end of the activity.

OSHA: _____
_____
_____

_____ 1. Provide health and safety-related training.

_____ 2. Use or wear prescribed protective equipment.

_____ 3. Make sure employees have and use safe tools and equipment.

_____ 4. Post signs to warn of potential hazards.

_____ 5. Comply with all standards.

_____ 6. Provide a workplace free from recognized hazards that could cause death or serious physical harm.

_____ 7. Report hazardous conditions to supervisor.

_____ 8. Read the OSHA poster.

_____ 9. Comply with all standards, rules, and regulations under OSHA.

_____ 10. Establish and update safe operating procedures.

_____ 11. Report job-related injuries or illnesses to a supervisor or management.

_____ 12. Keep records of work-related injuries and illnesses.

_____ 13. Follow all employer safety and health rules.

As a future employee, how do you believe OSHA will protect you? _____
_____
_____

Computers in Textiles and Apparel

Activity C   **Name** _____

Chapter 5   **Date** _____   **Period** _____

Complete the following statements using terms related to computers and apparel. Write your answers in the space provided.

cobalt88/Shutterstock.com

_____ 1. Workers using computer-aided ____ (CAM) software control the steps in producing finished textiles and garments.

_____ 2. Computers control ____ machines to automatically assemble and package complete garments.

_____ 3. Design software that has three-dimensional capabilities allows designers to turn a virtual ____ on the display screen to be viewed at any angle.

_____ 4. When the computer operator is satisfied with the pattern layout on the screen, a full-scale ____ is made.

_____ 5. Quick Response requires better ____ among companies at all levels.

_____ 6. Computer-____ manufacturing (CIM) helps coordinate the entire production process from design to finished product.

_____ 7. Computer-aided ____ (CAD) software is used to create textile and garment designs.

_____ 8. A ____ is a full-scale printout that is used as a cutting guide.

_____ 9. Different computer ____ throughout a manufacturing plant feed information into the main system.

Chapter 5   The Worldwide Apparel Industry   39

Worldwide Apparel Industry Review

Activity D   Name _____

Chapter 5   Date _____   Period _____

Complete the following statements about the worldwide apparel industry. Write your answers in the space provided.

_____ 1. ____ is the flow of goods, services, money, labor, and technology across international borders.

_____ 2. Goods that are sent out of a country are called ____.

_____ 3. Goods that come into a country from international sources are called ____.

_____ 4. A country's ____ ____ ____ is the difference between the values of its imports and its exports.

_____ 5. When the value of exports exceeds the value of imports, a ____ ____ exists.

_____ 6. A ____ ____ is a negative trade balance.

_____ 7. ____ limit how much of a good can be imported.

_____ 8. ____ are taxes governments assess on imports that make them more expensive for consumers to buy.

_____ 9. ____ is choosing how, when, and where a company will manufacture its goods or purchase its products.

_____ 10. ____ ____ occurs within a given country.

_____ 11. If a company looks beyond U.S. borders, this becomes ____ ____.

_____ 12. When a company chooses to produce its products outside its borders using its own production guidelines, ____ ____ occurs.

_____ 13. A ____ refers to a manufacturing plant that may use child labor, pay lower than minimum wages, not pay overtime, or have unclean or unsafe facilities.

_____ 14. The ____ ____ ____ ____ established a minimum wage and a maximum workweek of 40 hours.

_____ 15. ____ is the process of converting waste material or unwanted existing products into new products.

_____ 16. ____ ____ are natural resources—such as trees and plants—that nature can replenish.

_____ 17. ____ ____ are natural resources that can be used up. Nature cannot replenish them.

_____ 18. ____ are the moral principles that govern the behavior of a group or person.

_____ 19. ____ ____ are products that may appear identical to legitimate products, but the original manufacturer did not make them.

_____ 20. ____-____ involves conducting transactions electronically and online.

Chapter 6
A Closer Look at Fashion Design

You, the Designer

Activity A   Name _____

Chapter 6   Date _____ Period _____

Presume you have a career as a fashion designer. Give a brief description of your design philosophy. Then answer the following questions. Write your answers in the space provided.

My design philosophy: _____
_____
_____

1. Are your designs ready-to-wear or couture? Explain. _____
   _____
   _____

2. As a designer, what is your opinion about knockoffs of your designs? _____
   _____
   _____

3. As a designer, how do you think licensing your designs might benefit you? _____
   _____
   _____

4. For what categories and price points are your designs targeted? _____
   _____
   _____

5. Where do you work? _____
   _____
   _____

6. Where do you find inspiration for your designs? _____
   _____
   _____

Copyright Goodheart-Willcox Co., Inc. May not be reproduced or posted to a publicly accessible website.

Featured Fashion Designer

Activity B   **Name** _____

Chapter 6   **Date** _____ **Period** _____

Choose a fashion designer. Use fashion magazines or Internet sources to learn about the designer's biography and types of designs. Find pictures of the designs and paste copies of the images or the URL addresses in the space provided. Give an oral presentation of your findings in class.

Designer: _____

Brief biography: _____
_____
_____
_____
_____
_____
_____
_____
_____

Types of designs: _____
_____
_____

Communicating Fashion News

Activity C   **Name** _____

Chapter 6   **Date** _____   **Period** _____

Refer to the designs described in either Activity A or B. Describe how you might use the following technologies to communicate with potential customers about the designs. Write your responses in the space provided.

I would use the following technologies to communicate about the designs in Activity _____.

Websites: _____
_____
_____

Blogs: _____
_____
_____

YouTube: _____
_____
_____

Apps: _____
_____
_____

Twitter: _____
_____
_____

Facebook: _____
_____
_____

Television Shows: _____
_____
_____

Other: _____
_____
_____

Exploring a Trade Association

Activity D   **Name** _____

Chapter 6   **Date** _____   **Period** _____

Using Internet sources or current trade journals, research a textile and apparel industry trade association. Provide answers to the following questions in the space provided.

Name of trade association: _____

What is the purpose of this association? _____

_____

_____

_____

_____

How many members are in this association? _____

What are the membership requirements of this trade association? _____

_____

_____

_____

_____

_____

What functions does this trade association perform? _____

_____

_____

_____

_____

_____

If you had a career in the textile and apparel industry, would you consider joining this trade association? Explain. _____

_____

_____

_____

_____

Chapter 7

Planning a Wardrobe

Wardrobe Inventory

Activity A   **Name** _____

Chapter 7   **Date** _____ **Period** _____

Complete the clothing inventory chart that follows.

List of My Clothes	Description	How I Like It	Condition	What I Need to Add or Do

Copyright Goodheart-Willcox Co., Inc. May not be reproduced or posted to a publicly accessible website.

Clothing Wants

Activity B   **Name** _____

Chapter 7   **Date** _____   **Period** _____

Make a list of your clothing wants in the space that follows. Number them in order of importance to you. (Begin by writing the number 1 beside the most important want.)

_____
_____
_____
_____
_____
_____
_____
_____
_____
_____
_____
_____
_____
_____
_____
_____
_____
_____
_____
_____
_____
_____
_____
_____
_____
_____

How can attractive store displays cause you to confuse your clothing wants and needs?

_____
_____
_____
_____

Mixing and Matching

Activity C   **Name** _____

Chapter 7   **Date** _____ **Period** _____

Choose a color you could use as a foundation for a mix-and-match wardrobe. Then review online or print magazines and catalogs for garments you could use for at least four outfits in a mix-and-match wardrobe. Paste a copy of the images or the URL addresses in the space provided.

Foundation color: _____

Chapter 7   Planning a Wardrobe

Accessory Wardrobe

Activity D   Name _____

Chapter 7   Date _____   Period _____

Complete the following accessory charts. Identify accessories you own and their descriptions and accessories you need to add to your wardrobe and their descriptions. (Accessories include belts, jewelry, scarves, hats, neckties, handbags, and shoes.) Then answer the question that follows.

My Accessories	Description

Accessories I Need to Add	Description

What are the advantages of using accessories? _____

_____

_____

_____

_____

_____

Selecting Appropriate Clothes

Activity E Name _____

Chapter 7 Date _____ Period _____

Look through magazines, catalogs, or online sources to find pictures of clothes that are appropriate for the following situations. Keep in mind that these clothes should express your personality. Paste a copy of the images or the URL addresses in the spaces provided. Compare your choices with those of other class members.

Clothes you might wear to a football game:

Clothes you might wear on a date to the movies:

Clothes you might wear to a place of worship:

(Continued)

Activity E, continued   Name_____

Clothes you might wear to school:

[ ]

Clothes you would wear to a job interview:

[ ]

Clothes you might wear on a trip to _____:

[ ]

(Continued)

Activity E, continued   Name_____

Clothes you might wear to a formal *black tie* event:

Clothes you wear to do yard work:

Clothes you might wear to work in an office:

(Continued)

Activity E, continued   Name_____

Clothes you would wear to a wedding:

```
┌─────────────────────────────────────────────────────────────┐
│                                                             │
│                                                             │
│                                                             │
│                                                             │
└─────────────────────────────────────────────────────────────┘
```

Clothes you would wear to a funeral:

```
┌─────────────────────────────────────────────────────────────┐
│                                                             │
│                                                             │
│                                                             │
│                                                             │
└─────────────────────────────────────────────────────────────┘
```

Chapter 8: Apparel Decisions and Choices

Using the Decision-Making Process

Activity A   **Name** _____

Chapter 8   **Date** _____ **Period** _____

Make a clothing decision using the steps in the decision-making process outlined as follows. Write your responses in the space provided.

1. State the problem to be solved. _____
   _____

2. Set goals for what you want to accomplish. _____
   _____
   _____

3. Identify your resources. _____
   _____
   _____

4. List the alternatives. _____
   _____
   _____

5. Make your decision. (What decision have you made?) _____
   _____
   _____

6. Carry out the decision. (Explain how you will do this.) _____
   _____
   _____

7. Evaluate the results of the decision. _____
   _____
   _____

Factors Affecting Family Clothing Decisions

Activity B Name _____

Chapter 8 Date _____ Period _____

Interview a family. Describe the family and then find out the answers to the following questions. Share your interview responses with the class. Out of respect for the family, avoid using their real names.

Family Description:
_____
_____
_____
_____

1. How does your stage in the family life cycle affect family clothing decisions? _____
   _____
   _____

2. How do your family values, goals, and priorities influence clothing decisions? _____
   _____
   _____

3. How do your family resources affect clothing decisions? _____
   _____
   _____

4. How does your family budget affect clothing decisions? _____
   _____
   _____

5. What are some of the most successful family clothing decisions you have made? _____
   _____
   _____

6. How do you think you could improve your family clothing decisions? _____
   _____
   _____

7. What advice would you give to other families facing family clothing decisions? _____
   _____
   _____

Wardrobe Additions

Activity C   Name _____

Chapter 8   Date _____ Period _____

Presume you have a $400.00 wardrobe budget for the year (or ask your teacher for a dollar amount with which to work). Use online or print catalogs to make a list of items that you need or want to add to your wardrobe based on the clothing inventory you compiled earlier. Be sure to include indoor and outdoor wear, accessories, and shoes.

Clothing budget: $_____

Item and brief descriptions	Cost
	Total: $

Were you able to stay within the established budget? If not, what adjustments can you make to stay on budget?

_____

_____

_____

To Sew or to Buy

Activity D   **Name** _____

Chapter 8   **Date** _____ **Period** _____

Describe a garment you would like to own. Then answer the following questions. After answering the questions, use the decision-making process to decide whether you would sew or buy the garment.

Garment description: _____
_____

Ask yourself these questions:

1. How would you rate your sewing skills?
   _____ Excellent   _____ Good   _____ Fair   _____ Poor

2. How much money will it cost to make the garment? _____

3. How much money will it cost to buy the garment at a store? _____

4. How do the current fashions in the stores look on you? _____
   _____

5. Would you rather wear a personal, original design? _____

6. Do you see sewing as a fun activity or a chore? _____

7. Do you wear a standard size that requires little, if any, alterations? _____
   _____

8. Are you *in between* sizes? _____

9. Do you find that ready-made garments just do not fit you like they should? _____
   _____

10. When do you need the garment? _____

11. What would require the most time—shopping for the garment or sewing the garment? _____
    _____

12. Do you have enough time to shop for a pattern, fabric, and notions to make the garment? _____
    _____

Analyze your responses to the questions above. Using the decision-making process, make your decision. Then complete the following statement.

I have decided to _____ (sew, buy) this garment because _____
_____
_____
_____
_____

Chapter 9

Consumer Rights and Responsibilities

Using Labels

Activity A   Name _____

Chapter 9   Date _____ Period _____

Bring an article of clothing to class. Respond to the following statements and questions in the space provided.

1. List the information you find on the care label. _____
   _____
   _____

2. Is this garment machine washable, hand washable, or dry-cleanable? _____
   _____

3. What water temperature (hot, warm, cold) should you use for washing? _____
   _____

4. At what temperature (hot, warm, cool) should you dry the garment? _____
   _____

5. What information does the label give about bleaching? _____
   _____
   _____

6. What information does the label give about ironing? _____
   _____
   _____

7. Does the clothing care label include all the required information? If not, what is missing?
   _____
   _____

8. Predict what might happen if you did not follow the instructions on the clothing care label.
   _____
   _____

Generic Names and Trademark Names

Activity B   **Name** _____

Chapter 9   **Date** _____   **Period** _____

Match the generic names in the right column to their trademark names in the left column. Write your answer in the space provided. (*Note*: Some generic names will be used more than once.)

Trademark Names:

_____ 1. Creslan
_____ 2. MicroSafe
_____ 3. Dacron
_____ 4. Antron
_____ 5. Bemberg
_____ 6. Glospan
_____ 7. Estron
_____ 8. Wear-Dated
_____ 9. Anso
_____ 10. Lycra
_____ 11. Fortrel
_____ 12. Acrilan
_____ 13. Zantrel
_____ 14. Coolmax
_____ 15. Celanese
_____ 16. Herculon
_____ 17. Duraspun
_____ 18. Microlux
_____ 19. Tencel
_____ 20. Modal
_____ 21. Chromspun
_____ 22. Zeftron
_____ 23. SEF
_____ 24. Spectra
_____ 25. Enka

Generic Names:

A. Acetate
B. Acrylic
C. Lyocell
D. Modacrylic
E. Nylon
F. Olefin
G. Polyester
H. Rayon (viscose)
I. Spandex

Labeling Legislation

Activity C   **Name** _____

Chapter 9   **Date** _____ **Period** _____

Answer the following questions about clothing labels. Write your answers in the space provided.

1. By law, what must be stated on clothing labels? _____
   _____
   _____

2. What other information may be listed on a clothing label? _____
   _____
   _____

3. What is the difference between a label and a hangtag? _____
   _____
   _____

4. List three regulations dealing with clothing that are discussed in the text. Briefly describe each regulation in your own words.
   _____
   _____
   _____
   _____
   _____
   _____
   _____
   _____

5. What would you do if you could not find a label on a garment you wanted to buy? _____
   _____
   _____
   _____

Labeling

Activity D   **Name** _____

Chapter 9   **Date** _____   **Period** _____

Look through magazines or use Internet sources to find a picture of a garment. Paste a copy of the image or the URL address in the space provided. Briefly describe the garment, and write what information should be included on the label that might accompany the garment. Then, answer the question that follows.

Garment:

Label:

Description: _____
_____
_____

Does your label comply with government regulations? Explain. _____
_____
_____
_____

Consumer Complaint

Activity E **Name** _____

Chapter 9 **Date** _____ **Period** _____

Describe a problem you (or a member of your family) have had with a recent garment purchase. Then answer the following questions in the space provided. On the following page, write a letter to the store or manufacturer using the chapter guidelines.

Complaint: _____

_____

_____

_____

_____

_____

_____

_____

_____

What action was taken? _____

_____

_____

_____

_____

_____

_____

_____

_____

Was the problem handled fairly? Explain. _____

_____

_____

_____

_____

_____

_____

_____

_____

Explain why it is your responsibility to complain if a product does not perform as it should. _____

_____

_____

(Continued)

Activity E, continued Name_____

Your Sample Complaint Letter

Chapter 10

Choices as a Consumer

Where to Shop for Clothes

Activity A   **Name** _____

Chapter 10   **Date** _____ **Period** _____

Compare various shopping sources for clothes by completing the chart that follows. Then answer the question that follows the chart.

Shopping Sources and Names	Quality	Selection	Prices	Convenience	Other: (advantages and disadvantages)
Department Stores:					
Specialty Shops:					
Chain Stores:					
Discount Stores:					
Factory Outlet Stores:					
Resale Shops:					
Catalog Shopping:					
Online Shopping:					
Television Shopping:					
Personal Selling:					

(Continued)

Activity A, continued Name _____

From which source do you prefer to shop? Explain why. _____

Shopping Strategies

Activity B   **Name** _____

Chapter 10   **Date** _____ **Period** _____

Determine whether the following students are using good or poor clothing shopping strategies. Then explain your answer in the space provided.

1. Keshia sits down with a pencil and paper and outlines what she already has and what she needs to update her wardrobe.

    Good strategy? _____ Poor strategy? _____ Explain. _____
    _____
    _____
    _____

2. Bob does not skimp on important things like a coat or shoes he wears often.

    Good strategy? _____ Poor strategy? _____ Explain. _____
    _____
    _____
    _____

3. Ann buys something every time she goes shopping whether she needs it or not.

    Good strategy? _____ Poor strategy? _____ Explain. _____
    _____
    _____
    _____

4. Jerry makes quick and easy things himself. He saves his money to buy suits, jackets, and sweaters.

    Good strategy? _____ Poor strategy? _____ Explain. _____
    _____
    _____
    _____

5. Noah keeps his wardrobe down to two or three basic colors so everything can mix-and-match.

    Good strategy? _____ Poor strategy? _____ Explain. _____
    _____
    _____
    _____

(Continued)

Activity B, continued   Name_____

6. Cassandra buys clothes without considering the care they will require. She now has several outfits that require dry cleaning.

   Good strategy? _____ Poor strategy? _____ Explain. _____
   _____
   _____

7. Lorenzo only buys new merchandise at stores because he cannot wait for out-of-season sales.

   Good strategy? _____ Poor strategy? _____ Explain. _____
   _____
   _____

8. Sue has found one brand of jeans that fits her well. She intends to buy this brand again.

   Good strategy? _____ Poor strategy? _____ Explain. _____
   _____
   _____

9. Patrice refuses to buy clothes that need too many alterations.

   Good strategy? _____ Poor strategy? _____ Explain. _____
   _____
   _____

10. Pete buys clothes on impulse.

    Good strategy? _____ Poor strategy? _____ Explain. _____
    _____
    _____

In the space provided, list some of your buying strategies. Indicate whether they are good or poor.
_____
_____
_____
_____

Advertising

Activity C   **Name** _____

Chapter 10   **Date** _____ **Period** _____

Look through magazines or use Internet sources to find a clothing advertisement that appeals to you. Paste a copy of the advertisement or the URL address in the space provided. Then, respond to the questions and statement that follow.

```
┌─────────────────────────────────────────────────────────────┐
│                                                             │
│                                                             │
│                                                             │
│                                                             │
│                                                             │
│                                                             │
│                                                             │
│                                                             │
│                                                             │
│                                                             │
└─────────────────────────────────────────────────────────────┘
```

1. Why does this advertisement appeal to you? _____
   _____
   _____

2. What does this advertisement tell you about the item it is advertising? _____
   _____
   _____

3. Based upon this advertisement, I would _____
   _____
   _____

Consumer Shopping Terms

Activity D   Name _____

Chapter 10   Date _____ Period _____

Complete the following statements by writing your answer in the space provided to the left of each number.

_____ 1. Comparing qualities and prices in different retailers before buying is called ____ ____.

_____ 2. ____ ____ occurs when people buy something as soon as they see it, without stopping to think about their needs.

_____ 3. Television ____ advertise a product under the guise of a product demonstration by a host or expert.

_____ 4. ____ attempt to hide advertising by presenting it in the form of a newspaper article or magazine story.

_____ 5. A sale is a ____ only when consumers save money on items they need.

_____ 6. ____ ____ are planned when a store wants to sell items to make room for new merchandise.

_____ 7. ____ ____ are held before stock is counted or after it is counted.

_____ 8. ____-____-____ ____ are held to make room for new merchandise for a new season.

_____ 9. ____ ____ allow customers to receive discounts on the last ticketed prices.

_____ 10. ____-____ ____ feature items that are ahead of the season, such as coats sold at the end of summer.

_____ 11. ____-____ ____ offer products that were bought especially for these sales.

_____ 12. ____ ____ ____ are for people who have charge accounts with a specific retailer.

_____ 13. ____-____-____-____ ____ indicate that store owners are closing their businesses for some reason.

_____ 14. A ____ ____ is the price you pay for credit.

_____ 15. When you use a ____ ____, money is immediately deducted electronically from your bank account.

_____ 16. Buying on ____ is a promise to pay in the future for what you buy today.

_____ 17. With a ____ ____ ____, you may charge purchases in exchange for your promise to pay in full within 10 to 30 days after the billing date.

_____ 18. A ____ ____ ____ allows you to make purchases up to a limit set by the creditor when the account was opened.

_____ 19. An ____ is an advertising message paid for by an identified sponsor.

_____ 20. ____ ____ allows a store's customers to place small deposits on purchases that the store then holds for them.

68   *Apparel: Design, Textiles & Construction*   Workbook

Get Your Money's Worth

Quality Counts

Activity A Name _____

Chapter 11 Date _____ Period _____

Bring a garment you have purchased to class. Describe it and then analyze it by rating the garment on the score sheet that follows.

Garment description: _____
_____
_____

Signs of quality:	Excellent	Good	Fair	Poor
Good fit.				
Style looks attractive.				
Comfort.				
Easy care.				
Cost within budget.				
Color is becoming.				
Color combines with other clothes.				
Suitable for activities.				
Stripes, plaids, checks, and other designs matched at seams.				
Fabric free from flaws or irregularities.				
Fabric is appropriate for garment type and style.				
Garment pieces cut with the grain.				
Generous allowances for seams.				
Double row stitching to reinforce stress points, such as underarm seams, crotch, waist, neckline.				

(Continued)

69

Activity A, continued   Name_____

Signs of quality:	Excellent	Good	Fair	Poor
Smooth side seams and darts.				
Seams are flat, even in width, and wide enough to withstand strain and permit alterations.				
Raw edges finished.				
Stitching is short, continuous, and straight.				
Stitching securely fastened at the ends.				
Thread of the right weight, color, and fiber for the fabric.				
Extra stitching, bar tacks, metal rivets, or tape at points of strain.				
Hem is flat, even in width, invisible on right side.				
Buttonholes are smooth and properly placed.				
Buttonholes are firmly stitched and trimmed with no loose threads or frayed edges.				
Buttons, hooks and eyes, and snaps are firmly attached and properly spaced.				
Trim and decoration are suited to garment and have same care requirements as garment.				
Zippers and closures are securely stitched and easy to operate.				
Linings are smooth and properly inserted.				
Interfacing is properly hidden and securely attached.				
Pockets are flat, smooth, and properly matched to garment.				
Collars do not curl.				
Collar top is slightly turned over undercollar around seam edges.				
Lapels lay flat with smooth edge.				

What overall quality rating would you give this garment? Explain._____

_____

_____

_____

Inspecting for Quality

Activity B   Name _____

Chapter 11   Date _____   Period _____

Inspect three pairs of new jeans at a department store. The jeans should vary in brand, price, and quality. Assign a rating for each pair you inspect in the space provided. Then answer the following questions.

Use the following scale to rate the jeans:

    Excellent   = 4
    Good   = 3
    Fair   = 2
    Poor   = 1
    Does not apply = NA

	Jeans		
	A	B	C
Brand:			
1. Jeans have a hangtag or attached label that tells fiber content and how to care for the jeans.			
2. Jeans are preshrunk.			
3. If jeans will fade, special instructions are given.			
4. Stitching is well done with suitable color thread.			
5. Zipper—heavy-duty and securely stitched.			
6. Pockets securely attached with reinforced stitching or rivets at corners and tops.			
7. Seams—double-stitched or flat-felled and no signs of puckering.			
8. Snap or button easy to close.			
9. Buttonhole firmly stitched.			
10. Jeans will require a minimum of care.			

1. Compare the different pairs of jeans. What are the positive and negative qualities of each pair of jeans?

    A. _____

    _____

    _____

    B. _____

    _____

    _____

(Continued)

Activity B, continued   Name _____

    C. _____
_____
_____
_____

2. How do the jeans compare in price?

    A. _____

    B. _____

    C. _____

3. Which pair of jeans would you buy? Explain why. _____
_____
_____
_____

4. Which pair of jeans would you avoid buying? Explain why. _____
_____
_____
_____
_____

5. How can evaluating these jeans relate to other garments you may buy? _____
_____
_____
_____
_____
_____
_____
_____
_____
_____
_____
_____

Making the Most of Accessories

Activity C **Name** _____

Chapter 11 **Date** _____ **Period** _____

Look through magazines or use Internet sources to find a picture of a basic outfit, as well as pictures of accessories that you could use with this outfit. Paste a copy of the images or the URL addresses in the space provided. Compare and discuss your examples in class

My Preferences

Activity D   Name _____

Chapter 11   Date _____   Period _____

Choose the statement that best describes your feelings. Answer the question that follows the statements and write the letter in the space provided.

_____ 1. A. I'm always on the lookout for low-cost clothing. I like to have many outfits from which to choose, otherwise I get bored with my wardrobe.

         B. I would rather spend a little more for quality clothes and have only a few outfits.

_____ 2. A. I try to choose fabrics and styles that can be worn all year and through several seasons.

         B. I like the summer cottons and the winter wools. I change with the weather.

_____ 3. A. Because my weight changes, I need my clothes to be adjustable, so I look for elastic waists in clothes.

         B. It is not necessary for my clothes to be adjustable because my weight does not change much.

_____ 4. A. I'm an athletic person. My clothing must always be comfortable and allow for movement.

         B. Sometimes I'm willing to sacrifice comfort for fashion.

_____ 5. A. I like neutral colors that will coordinate with many other colors.

         B. I like bright colors. I also like mixing up unusual colors to make different combinations.

_____ 6. A. I need clothing that requires easy care. I'll do anything to keep from ironing.

         B. I'm willing to spend extra time caring for my clothes. I do not mind some hand-washing and ironing.

_____ 7. A. I enjoy wearing designer clothing.

         B. Designer names are not important to me. I buy clothes that look good and are of high quality.

_____ 8. A. I like to buy clothes that are in classic styles. I know that I can wear them next year and still feel comfortable.

         B. I'm always first to try new fashions. I love the *in* styles.

_____ 9. A. When buying shoes, comfort is the most important consideration to me.

         B. Fashion is the most important consideration to me when I buy shoes.

_____ 10. A. I like to dress up my outfits with accessories. I shop carefully for accessories to match my outfits.

         B. It's too much trouble to worry about extras. I seldom shop for accessories to match my outfits.

How can you use this information as you plan your clothing purchases? _____

_____

_____

_____

_____

Chapter 12 — Selecting Apparel for Family Members

Choosing Clothes for Family Members

Activity A Name _____

Chapter 12 Date _____ **Period** _____

Presume you are shopping for each of the people described in the following. Look through catalogs or magazines to find appropriate pictures of clothes for each person. Paste a copy of the images of URL addresses in the spaces provided. Identify a reason for each of your selections.

Baby: boy or girl, 3 months old

Reason for selection:

_____

Toddler: girl or boy, 2 years old

Reason for selection:

_____

(Continued)

Activity A, continued Name_____

Preschooler: boy or girl, 4 years old

Reason for selection:

_____

School-age child: girl or boy, 8 years old

Reason for selection:

_____

(Continued)

Activity A, continued   Name_____

Teen: guy or girl, 15 years old

Reason for selection:

_____

Adult: female or male teacher

Reason for selection:

_____

(Continued)

Activity A, continued   Name_____

Retired person: male or female who enjoys traveling

Reason for selection:
_____

Person with a physical disability: a teen (female or male) with limited hand movement who uses a wheelchair

Reason for selection:
_____

Selecting Clothes for Children

Activity B   **Name** _____

Chapter 12   **Date** _____ **Period** _____

Invite a panel of parents to class who have children of various ages. Ask the parents the following questions. Write their responses in the space provided.

1. What is the most important consideration in selecting clothes for:

    babies? _____
    _____

    toddlers? _____
    _____

    preschoolers? _____
    _____

    school-age children? _____
    _____

2. What types of clothes are worn most often by:

    babies? _____
    _____

    toddlers? _____
    _____

    preschoolers? _____
    _____

    school-age children? _____
    _____

3. What safety features should be included in clothes for:

    babies? _____
    _____

    toddlers? _____
    _____

    preschoolers? _____
    _____

    school-age children? _____
    _____

Clothes for People with Physical Disabilities

Activity C   Name _____

Chapter 12   Date _____   Period _____

Interview a physical therapist or a nursing home worker to discuss the needs of people with various types of physical disabilities. List four types of physical disabilities in the left column of the following chart. In the right column, list types of clothes that should be selected for a person with this physical disability or adaptations that can be made to clothes to make them suitable for him or her.

Physical Disability	Clothing Needs or Adaptations

Chapter 13 Keeping Apparel Looking Its Best

Clothing Care Do's and Don'ts

Activity A Name _____

Chapter 13 Date _____ Period _____

Read the following statements. If a statement describes something that should be done when caring for clothes, place a check in the *Do* column. If a statement describes something that should *not* be done, place a check in the *Don't* column.

Do	Don't	
____	____	1. At the end of the day, toss clothes onto a chair.
____	____	2. Check clothes for stains and do some preliminary stain removal.
____	____	3. Place heavier garments on padded hangers or wide, shaped wood or plastic hangers.
____	____	4. Hang sweaters on hangers.
____	____	5. Empty all pockets.
____	____	6. Leave zippers unzipped and buttons unbuttoned.
____	____	7. Place soiled clothing items in drawers to keep them out of sight.
____	____	8. Use a clothes brush or lint roller to brush dust and lint off garments.
____	____	9. Treat a stain as soon as you see it.
____	____	10. Iron over a stain.
____	____	11. Take non-washable garments to the dry cleaner.
____	____	12. Hang slacks on a wire hanger.
____	____	13. Store seasonal clothing in a damp basement.
____	____	14. Store only clothing that is clean.
____	____	15. Have winter clothes dry-cleaned before storing them.
____	____	16. If garments must be stacked, place heavier items at the bottom.
____	____	17. If a garment has a loose button, wear the garment until the button falls off.
____	____	18. If a hem comes loose, repair the stitches before wearing the garment again.
____	____	19. Have a place designated for dirty laundry.
____	____	20. Store clothes in direct sunlight.

Stain Removal

Activity B   Name _____

Chapter 13   Date _____   **Period** _____

Complete the following stain removal chart. Write your answers in the space provided. (*Optional:* Test one or two of the procedures you have outlined below on scraps of fabric. Note how well the procedure worked for each sample.

Stain	Removal procedure
Adhesive tape	
Ballpoint ink	
Blood	
Candle wax	
Car grease, oil	
Chewing gum	
Chocolate	

(Continued)

82   *Apparel: Design, Textiles & Construction*   Workbook

Activity B, continued   Name _____

Stain	Removal procedure
Coffee or tea	
Cosmetics	
Deodorants or antiperspirants	
Grass	
Ice cream or milk	
Nail polish	
Fruit—fruit juices, soft drinks, punches	
Perspiration	
Scorch	

Comparing Laundry Products

Activity C   Name _____

Chapter 13   Date _____ Period _____

Complete the following chart about the laundry products you use to keep your clothes clean. Compare your chart with those of other class members.

	Laundry Product 1	**Laundry Product 2**	**Laundry Product 3**	**Laundry Product 4**
Product name:				
Directions for use:				
Cautions:				
Effectiveness:				
Cost of product and net contents:				
Helpful information about product:				

Chapter 14

Laundry and Dry Cleaning

Caring for Clothes

Activity A   **Name** _____

Chapter 14   **Date** _____   **Period** _____

Choose six items of clothing you frequently wear. Describe each item in the space provided. List the care label instructions. Then describe the procedure you use to care for each item.

1. Item: _____

   Care label instructions: _____
   _____
   _____
   _____

   To care for this item I: _____
   _____
   _____
   _____
   _____

2. Item: _____

   Care label instructions: _____
   _____
   _____
   _____

   To care for this item I: _____
   _____
   _____
   _____
   _____

(Continued)

Activity A, continued Name _____

3. Item: _____

   Care label instructions: _____
   _____
   _____

   To care for this item I: _____
   _____
   _____
   _____

4. Item: _____

   Care label instructions: _____
   _____
   _____

   To care for this item I: _____
   _____
   _____
   _____

5. Item: _____

   Care label instructions: _____
   _____
   _____

   To care for this item I: _____
   _____
   _____
   _____

6. Item: _____

   Care label instructions: _____
   _____
   _____

   To care for this item I: _____
   _____
   _____
   _____

Choose the Right Temperature

Activity B   Name _____

Chapter 14   Date _____   Period _____

Indicate the water temperature for hot, warm, and cold water. Then imagine you are washing the following items. Next to each item place a check in the column of the correct water temperature for washing the item or water temperature descriptions.

Hot water: ____ °F and above

Warm water: about ____ °F

Cold water: ____ °F

	Hot Water	Warm Water	Cold Water	
1.				Non-colorfast, lightly soiled items
2.				Silks
3.				Sturdy whites
4.				Washable woolens
5.				Diapers
6.				Colorfast items
7.				Moderately soiled, permanent press, and non-colorfast items
8.				Dark colored items that are lightly soiled
9.				Heavily soiled permanent press items
10.				Manufactured fibers
11.				Does best job of removing soil and disinfecting
12.				Helps conserve energy
13.				Increases wrinkling
14.				Reduces wrinkling and color fading
15.				Can cause garments to shrink
16.				Produces less shrinkage, color loss, and wrinkling
17.				Can cause colors to run

Professional Dry Cleaning

Activity C Name _____

Chapter 14 Date _____ Period _____

Visit a local dry cleaner. Find out the answers to the following questions. Write your answers in the space provided.

1. What are the consumer's responsibilities when bringing garments to a dry cleaner? _____
   _____
   _____
   _____

2. What happens during the dry-cleaning process? Describe the dry-cleaning process. _____
   _____
   _____
   _____

3. What are the average costs for dry cleaning the following garments?

   Sport coat: _____

   Dress: _____

   Suit: _____

   Pants: _____

   Skirt: _____

   Sweater: _____

   Coat: _____

   Other items: _____
   _____

4. What other services are offered by a dry cleaner? Describe them. _____
   _____
   _____
   _____
   _____
   _____
   _____
   _____

Apparel: Design, Textiles & Construction Workbook

Chapter 15: Repair, Redesign, and Recycle

Keeping Your Clothes Wearable

Activity A   **Name** _____

Chapter 15   **Date** _____ **Period** _____

Answer the following questions about repairing clothes. Write your answers in the space provided.

1. If you have clothes that need repairs, what should you do with them? _____
   _____

2. What is patching? _____
   _____

3. What are two advantages of using a sewing machine rather than hand sewing to repair a garment? _____
   _____
   _____

4. What type of stitch can you use to repair sweaters and other knitted garments? _____
   _____

5. What might happen if you delay a repair job until after laundering a garment? _____
   _____
   _____

6. If you do not have the exact color of thread for a repair job, should you use a darker shade or a lighter one? _____
   _____

7. Why is a second row of stitches often used to repair a seam in the seat of slacks? _____
   _____

8. Why is it best to remove loose buttons when you first notice them? _____
   _____

9. Which items should you keep in a clothing repair box? _____
   _____

89

Copyright Goodheart-Willcox Co., Inc. May not be reproduced or posted to a publicly accessible website.

Altering for a Better Fit

Activity B Name _____

Chapter 15 Date _____ Period _____

Invite an alterations specialist from a department store or dry cleaner to demonstrate how to do various types of alterations on garments. Take notes in the spaces provided about special techniques used and alterations you may like to perform on some of your own clothes.

Altering length: _____

_____

_____

_____

_____

_____

_____

_____

_____

_____

_____

_____

_____

_____

_____

_____

Altering width: _____

_____

_____

_____

_____

_____

_____

_____

_____

_____

_____

_____

_____

_____

_____

Clothing Repair and Alterations

Activity C   **Name** _____

Chapter 15   **Date** _____   **Period** _____

In your own words, recommend the best way to repair or alter the following garments. Write your answers in the space provided.

1. Bill has a hole in the elbow of his jacket.

    Recommended repair: _____
    _____

2. Jane has a hole in the knee of her blue jeans.

    Recommended repair: _____
    _____

3. Terry has a small hole in the leg of her wool slacks.

    Recommended repair: _____
    _____

4. The seam in the seat of Tom's pants is ripped.

    Recommended repair: _____
    _____

5. The button on Mary's coat is loose.

    Recommended repair: _____
    _____

6. Julie's skirt is too long.

    Recommended repair: _____
    _____

7. Jim's pants are slightly too tight.

    Recommended repair: _____
    _____

8. The waistband on Rosa's blouse is too big.

    Recommended repair: _____
    _____

Redesigning and Recycling Ideas

Activity D   **Name** _____

Chapter 15   **Date** _____   **Period** _____

Look through your closet. List garments you no longer wear in the left column of the following chart. Think of ideas of your own or use Internet or print resources to find ideas for redesigning or recycling these clothes.

Garment	Redesigning or Recycling Idea

Chapter 16

Reactions to Color

Activity A   Name _____

Chapter 16   Date _____ Period _____

People react differently to colors. The following list includes various colors. Give your reaction to each color. Compare your reactions with those of others in the class and record some of your classmate's reactions. Then answer the questions that follow your reactions in the space provided.

Red

Your reaction: _____

Classmate's reaction: _____

Orange

Your reaction: _____

Classmate's reaction: _____

Yellow

Your reaction: _____

Classmate's reaction: _____

Green

Your reaction: _____

Classmate's reaction: _____

Blue

Your reaction: _____

Classmate's reaction: _____

Purple

Your reaction: _____

Classmate's reaction: _____

(Continued)

Activity A, continued Name_____

Black

Your reaction: _____

Classmate's reaction: _____

White

Your reaction: _____

Classmate's reaction: _____

1. Which colors are your favorite colors? Explain. _____
   _____
   _____
   _____

2. What are your least favorite colors? Explain. _____
   _____
   _____
   _____

3. Which colors do you like to wear most often? Explain. _____
   _____
   _____
   _____

4. Which colors would you rather not wear? Explain. _____
   _____
   _____
   _____

Color Basics

Activity B   Name _____

Chapter 16   Date _____   **Period** _____

Complete these statements about color by filling in the blanks. Then, look through magazines or use Internet sources to find color swatches of the primary, secondary, and tertiary colors. Paste a copy of the images or the URL addresses in the spaces provided.

_____ 1. The lightness or darkness of a color is its ____.

_____ 2. A ____ is made by adding white to a color.

_____ 3. A ____ is made by adding black to a color.

_____ 4. The brightness or dullness of a color is its ____.

_____ 5. The ____ ____ shows the relationship among colors or hues.

_____ 6. Red, yellow, and blue are ____ hues.

_____ 7. Orange, green, and violet are ____ hues.

_____ 8. Red-violet, blue-violet, blue-green, yellow-orange, and red-orange are ____ hues.

_____ 9. When many values of one color are used together, the color scheme is called ____.

_____ 10. Colors that are opposite each other on the color wheel, such as red and green, form a ____ color scheme.

_____ 11. When adjacent colors are used together, the color scheme is called ____.

_____ 12. Black, white, and gray are ____.

_____ 13. Reds and oranges are considered ____ colors because they are bright and cheerful, and they advance.

_____ 14. Blues and greens are considered ____ colors because they are restful and relaxing, and they recede.

(Continued)

Activity B, continued   Name_____

Primary colors:

Secondary colors:

Tertiary colors:

Color Schemes and Combinations

Activity C   **Name** _____

Chapter 16   **Date** _____   **Period** _____

Look through magazines or use Internet sources to find images of outfits that utilize the following color schemes and combinations. Paste a copy of the images or the URL addresses in the spaces provided.

Monochromatic color scheme:

Analogous color scheme:

Complementary color scheme:

(Continued)

Activity C, continued Name_____

Split-complementary color scheme:

Triadic color scheme:

Accented neutral color scheme:

Warm color combination:

Cool color combination:

Color and Your Clothes

Activity D Name _____

Chapter 16 Date _____ Period _____

Use your creativity in combining color and clothes to create two attractive outfits. Look through magazines, catalogs, or online for color pictures of various types of clothes, such as pants, skirts, shirts, and blouses, that would look good on you. Paste a copy of the images or the URL addresses in the spaces provided. Then answer the questions that follow.

1. How would the colors in these outfits go with your personal coloring? _____
   _____

2. How would the colors in these outfits go with your body type? _____
   _____

Color Trends

Activity E Name _____

Chapter 16 Date _____ Period _____

Look through print or online catalogs to find two examples of color trends featured this season. Paste a copy of the images of URL addresses in the spaces provided. Then answer the questions that follow.

1. What is your opinion of the current fashion colors? _____
   _____
   _____

2. How will these colors look on you? _____
   _____

Chapter 17: The Elements and Principles of Design

Basic Figure/Physique Types

Activity A   **Name** _____

Chapter 17   **Date** _____ **Period** _____

Identify the basic figure/physique types shown in the following. Then write one idea about how you could use the elements and principles of design to create an optical illusion to enhance the features of this figure/physique type. Write your answers in the space provided.

1. _____

2. _____

3. _____

4. _____

5. _____

101

Using the Elements of Design

Activity B   **Name** _____

Chapter 17   **Date** _____   **Period** _____

Look through magazines or use Internet sources to find an image of an outfit that would look good on you. Paste a copy of the image or the URL address in the space provided. Then, describe how the elements of design were used in the outfit.

Color: _____
_____
_____

Line: _____
_____
_____

Form and shape: _____
_____
_____

Texture: _____
_____
_____

Creating Illusions with Lines

Activity C   **Name** _____

Chapter 17   **Date** _____   **Period** _____

Look at the illustrations that follow. Lines have been drawn to create vertical or horizontal illusions. Indicate which lines would make a person look taller and more slender by writing *vertical* in the appropriate blanks. Indicate which lines would make a person look shorter and more rounded by writing *horizontal* in the appropriate blanks.

1. _____ 2. _____ 3. _____ 4. _____

5. _____ 6. _____ 7. _____ 8. _____

Which lines would look best on you? Explain. _____
_____
_____
_____

Chapter 17   The Elements and Principles of Design

Using the Principles of Design

Activity D   **Name** _____

Chapter 17   **Date** _____   **Period** _____

Look through magazines or use Internet sources to find pictures that show examples of each of the following principles of design. Paste a copy of the images or URL addresses in the spaces provided. Briefly describe how the principle was used in each design. Then, answer the question at the end of the activity.

Balance—Formal balance:

Balance—Informal balance:

(Continued)

Activity D, continued   Name_____

Rhythm—Repetition:

Rhythm—Gradation:

Rhythm—Radiation:

(Continued)

Activity D, continued Name_____

Proportion:

_____
_____
_____
_____
_____
_____
_____
_____
_____
_____

Emphasis:

_____
_____
_____
_____
_____
_____
_____
_____
_____
_____
_____
_____

Explain how the goal of harmony is achieved in a design. _____
_____
_____
_____
_____
_____

Chapter 18

The Natural Fibers

Fiber Fill-in-the-Blanks

Activity A   **Name** _____

Chapter 18   **Date** _____ **Period** _____

Complete the statements about fibers that follow. Write your answers in the space provided.

_____ 1. When fibers are put together to form a continuous strand, a ____ is made.

_____ 2. Yarns are woven or knitted together to make ____.

_____ 3. ____ ____ are made from natural sources—plants and animals.

_____ 4. ____ ____ are made from chemicals in factories.

_____ 5. ____ ____ come from vegetable (plant) sources.

_____ 6. ____ ____ come from animal sources.

_____ 7. ____ is the most widely used natural fiber.

_____ 8. ____ is a discoloration caused by a fungus that grows on some fabrics when they are moist for a period of time.

_____ 9. Flax is the fiber used to make ____ fabric.

_____ 10. ____ comes from a shrubby plant that grows often in China and India.

_____ 11. The main use of ____ is for making burlap bags, but it is also used for decorative household items and accessories.

_____ 12. ____ is made from the fleece (hair) of sheep or lambs.

_____ 13. Carded sliver is made into ____ ____ that use the short fibers (less than two inches).

_____ 14. Yarns made from combed sliver (called *top* in the case of wool) are called ____ ____.

_____ 15. To protect consumers and manufacturers, the ____ ____ ____ ____ was passed to help overcome confusion and misinformation about the wool used in products.

_____ 16. The term *wool* or ____ ____ means that the fiber has never been used before for a fabric or garment.

_____ 17. ____ ____ contains wool fibers from previously made wool fabrics.

_____ 18. ____ is a protein fiber that comes from the cocoons of silkworms.

Natural Fiber Facts

Activity B   Name _____

Chapter 18   Date _____   **Period** _____

Complete the following chart about natural fibers. Write your responses in the space provided.

Fibers	Care	Advantages	Disadvantages	Uses
Cotton				
Flax (Linen)				
Ramie				
Wool				
Silk				

Apparel: Design, Textiles & Construction   Workbook

Natural Fibers and Prices

Activity C   **Name** _____

Chapter 18   **Date** _____ **Period** _____

Visit a fabric store. Compare prices of various fabrics made from the fibers in the following list. Then respond to the statements and questions that follow the chart by writing your answers in the spaces provided.

Fiber	Width	Cost per yd. or m
Cotton		
Linen		
Ramie		
Wool		
Silk		

1. List the three most expensive fabrics. _____
_____
_____
_____
_____

2. Why do you suppose these fabrics are more expensive? _____
_____
_____
_____
_____

3. List the three least expensive fabrics. _____
_____
_____
_____

4. Why do you suppose these fabrics are least expensive? _____
_____
_____
_____
_____

Natural Fiber Research

Activity D   **Name** _____

Chapter 18   **Date** _____   **Period** _____

Research a natural fiber of your choice. In the space provided, prepare a report. Write a paragraph describing each of the items below.

Fiber: _____

Fiber history: _____

_____

_____

_____

Fiber characteristics: _____

_____

_____

_____

How the fiber is produced: _____

_____

_____

_____

Uses of the fiber: _____

_____

_____

_____

Other fiber facts: _____

_____

_____

Chapter 19: The Manufactured Fibers

Manufactured Fiber Facts

Activity A   Name _____

Chapter 19   Date _____ Period _____

Complete the following chart about manufactured fibers. Write your responses in the space provided.

Fibers	Care	Advantages	Disadvantages	Uses
Rayon				
Lyocell				
Acetate				
Triacetate				

(Continued)

Activity A, continued   Name_____

Fibers	Care	Advantages	Disadvantages	Uses
Nylon				
Polyester				
Olefin				
Acrylic				
Modacrylic				
Spandex				
Elastoester				

Manufactured Fibers and Prices

Activity B   Name _____

Chapter 19   Date _____   Period _____

Visit a fabric store. Compare prices of various fabrics made from the fibers in the following chart. Then respond to the statements and questions that follow the chart.

Fiber	Width	Cost per yd. or m
Rayon		
Lyocell		
Acetate		
Triacetate		
Nylon		
Polyester		
Olefin		
Acrylic		
Modacrylic		
Spandex		
Elastoester		

1. List the three most expensive fabrics and their prices. _____
   _____
   _____

2. Why do you suppose these fabrics are more expensive? _____
   _____
   _____

3. List the three least expensive fabrics and their prices. _____
   _____
   _____

4. Why do you suppose these fabrics are least expensive? _____
   _____
   _____

Manufactured Fiber Research

Activity C   **Name** _____

Chapter 19   **Date** _____ **Period** _____

Research a manufactured fiber of your choice. In the space provided, prepare a report. Write a paragraph describing each of the following items. Present your report to the class.

Fiber: _____

Fiber history: _____

_____
_____
_____
_____
_____

Fiber characteristics: _____

_____
_____
_____
_____
_____

How the fiber is produced: _____

_____
_____
_____
_____
_____

Uses of the fiber: _____

_____
_____
_____
_____

Other fiber facts: _____

_____
_____
_____
_____

Chapter 20

From Yarn to Fabric

Yarn and Fabric Term Review

Activity A   Name _____

Chapter 20   Date _____ Period _____

Complete the following statements using terms listed in the word bank that follows. Write your responses in the spaces provided.

blend	plain weave
bonding	ply yarn
combination yarn	quilting
cord yarn	satin weave
felt	selvage
filling yarns	single yarn
films	spun yarns
grain	twill weave
knitting	warp knitting
monofilament yarns	warp yarns
multifilament yarns	weaving
nap	weft knitting
pile fabric	woven fabric

1. _____ _____ are made from short, staple fibers.

2. _____ _____ are made from a single filament.

3. A group of filaments form _____ _____.

4. The product of the first twisting step is a _____ _____.

5. Twisting two or more single yarns together makes a _____ _____.

6. When ply yarns are twisted together, the result is a _____ _____.

7. When different types of staple fibers are spun together into a single yarn, the result is a _____.

8. _____ _____ result from twisting two or more different yarns into a ply.

(Continued)

115

Activity A, continued   Name_____

9. _____ is the process of interlacing yarns at right angles to each other.

10. Interlacing yarns at right angles to each other creates a _____ _____.

11. Lengthwise yarns are the _____ _____.

12. Crosswise yarns are the _____ _____.

13. The turned filling yarns along each side of the woven fabric form the _____—the fabric edge that is very strong and will not ravel.

14. _____ refers to the direction the yarns run.

15. Passing a filling yarn over one warp yarn and then under one warp yarn makes the _____ _____.

16. The _____ _____ forms when a yarn in one direction floats (passes) over two or more yarns in the other direction.

17. The _____ _____ forms by floating a yarn from one direction over four or more yarns from the other direction and then under one yarn.

18. A _____ _____ has ends or loops of yarn extending above the surface of the fabric.

19. The _____ is a layer of fiber ends above the fabric surface. The nap lies in one direction on a pile fabric.

20. _____ is a process that loops yarns together.

21. In _____ _____, the loops are made as yarn is added in the crosswise direction.

22. In _____ _____, the loops are made by one or more sets of warp yarns. Each set of warp yarns is as wide as the fabric.

23. _____ is made from short wool fibers.

24. _____, which are not made of fibers, are thin sheets of vinyl and urethane.

25. _____ is the process of permanently fastening (gluing) one fabric to another.

26. _____ is the process of adding a layer of padding (batting) between two layers of fabric.

Single, Ply, and Cord Yarns

Activity B Name _____

Chapter 20 Date _____ Period _____

Label the following illustrations of yarns. Then, explain the relationship among these yarns in the space provided.

1. _____   2. _____   3. _____

Explanation: _____
_____
_____
_____
_____
_____
_____
_____
_____
_____
_____
_____
_____
_____

Woven and Knitted Fabrics

Activity C   Name _____

Chapter 20   Date _____   Period _____

Look at the list of fabrics that follows. If a fabric is a woven one, write *W* in the blank. If the fabric is a knitted one, write *K* in the blank. Then name the type of weave (plain, twill, or satin) or the type of knit (weft or warp) used to produce the fabric.

1. Organdy _____
2. Herringbone _____
3. Double knit _____
4. Stockinette _____
5. Voile _____
6. Broadcloth _____
7. Serge _____
8. Tricot _____
9. Chiffon _____
10. Lace _____
11. Gabardine _____
12. Taffeta _____
13. Jersey _____
14. Muslin _____
15. Rib knit _____
16. Poplin _____
17. Raschel knit _____

18. Gingham _____
19. Knitted terry cloth _____
20. Surah _____
21. Percale _____
22. Velour _____
23. Grosgrain _____
24. Faille _____
25. Power net _____
26. Batiste _____
27. Fisherman's knit _____
28. Denim _____
29. Oxford _____
30. Purl knit _____
31. Flannel _____
32. Chambray _____
33. Satin _____
34. Sateen _____

Fabric Construction

Activity D   **Name** _____

Chapter 20   **Date** _____ **Period** _____

Close-up photographs of various types of fabric constructions are shown in the following. Identify each one. Then, look through magazines or use Internet sources to find pictures that show examples of each type of fabric construction. Paste a copy of the images or URL addresses in the spaces provided.

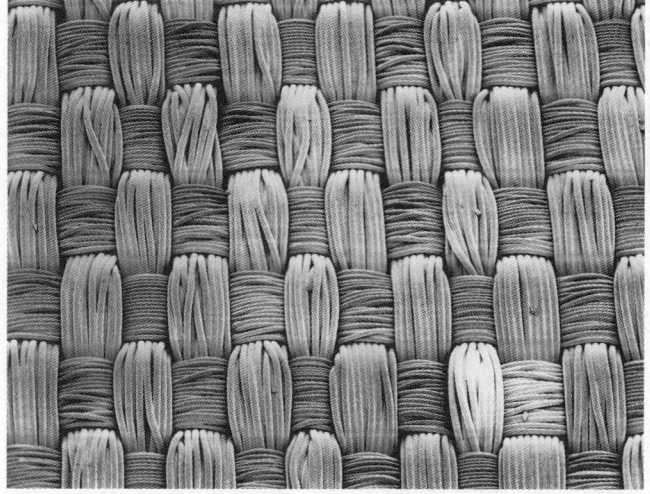

American Textile Manufacturers Institute

1. _____

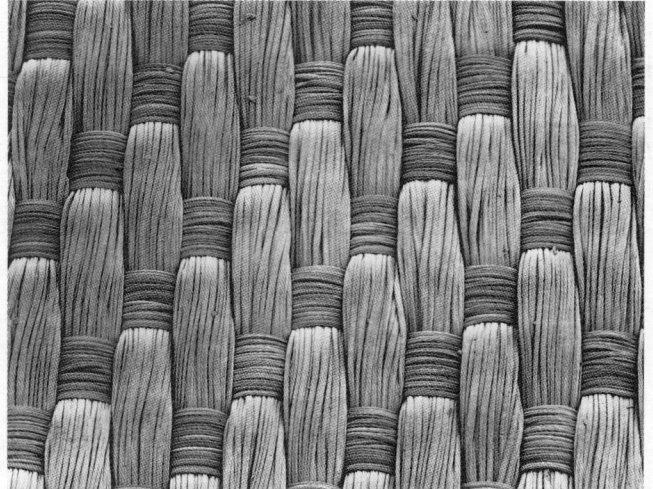

American Textile Manufacturers Institute

2. _____

(Continued)

Chapter 20   From Yarn to Fabric

Activity D, continued   Name_____

American Textile Manufacturers Institute

3. _____

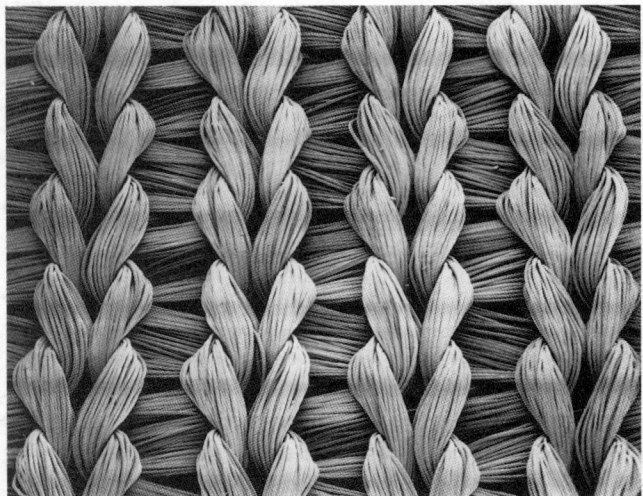
American Textile Manufacturers Institute

4. _____

Chapter 21
Fabric Color and Finishes

Textile Color and Finishes Technology

Activity A   **Name** _____

Chapter 21   **Date** _____ **Period** _____

Using online sources, research current textile color and finish technology. In the space that follows, write an article summarizing your findings and share it with the class.

_____
_____
_____
_____
_____
_____
_____
_____
_____
_____
_____
_____
_____
_____
_____
_____
_____
_____
_____
_____
_____
_____
_____

Adding Color to Textiles

Activity B   Name _____

Chapter 21   Date _____   **Period** _____

Complete the following statements by writing your answers in the blanks provided.

1. _____ are coloring agents that are used to add color to fibers, yarns, fabrics, or garments.

2. If fibers are dyed before they are spun into yarns, the process is _____.

3. In _____ _____, the dye is added to the thick liquid before it is forced through the spinneret.

4. In _____ _____, the dye is added to the loose fibers.

5. In _____ _____ after spinning, the yarns are tightly wound on tubes, and then placed in the dye bath.

6. During the _____ _____ process, color is added after the fabric has been made.

7. When placing a fabric consisting of more than one fiber in a dye bath, it can become a stripe or check, or other pattern through a _____-_____ process.

8. With _____ _____, an undyed finished garment is dyed after construction.

9. _____ means the color will remain in spite of a certain influence such as washing, dry cleaning, perspiration, sunlight, or rubbing.

10. _____ is the process of adding color, pattern, or design to fabric surfaces.

11. In _____ printing, the design is etched on copper rollers.

12. In _____ printing, a woven-mesh screen attached to a wooden frame suspends an ink-blocking stencil over the fabric.

13. _____ _____ printing combines both roller- and screen-printing methods.

14. In _____ _____ printing, the dyes are first printed on paper, then with the application of heat and pressure to the paper and fabric, the dyes change to gases that move from the paper base onto the fabric.

15. _____ printing creates printable designs on a computer that are then sent directly to fabric printing machinery.

Dyeing and Printing

Activity C **Name** _____

Chapter 21 **Date** _____ **Period** _____

Look through magazines or use Internet sources to find pictures that show examples of fabrics that have been dyed and printed. Paste a copy of the images or URL addresses in the spaces provided.

Chapter 21   Fabric Color and Finishes

Finishes

Activity D Name _____
Chapter 21 Date _____ Period _____

Match the following finishes with their descriptions. Write the letter of the correct response in the space provided.

_____ 1. Finishes that allow fabrics to be more easily wetted, helping detergents do their job.

_____ 2. Fabric is placed in an industrial washer that is filled with pumice stones, and as the cylinder rotates, the stones repeatedly beat against the fabric.

_____ 3. Fabrics have been processed so they will not shrink more than one percent in either direction when washed.

_____ 4. Finishes that cause fabrics to repel food, water, and other substances by reducing absorbency.

_____ 5. The application of heat and pressure with rollers on fabrics to produce a smooth, polished surface.

_____ 6. Helps fabrics resist wrinkles, but also makes fabrics weaker and less absorbent.

_____ 7. Involves the application of starch or resin to fabrics to increase weight, body, and luster.

_____ 8. Adding metallic salts to silk.

_____ 9. The colors remain true for a longer period of time.

_____ 10. This chemical finish works by cutting off the oxygen supply or changing the chemical makeup of the fibers, which causes the flame to extinguish itself.

_____ 11. A chemical treatment used on cotton and rayon fabrics to improve luster, strength, and absorbency.

_____ 12. This finish suppresses the growth of odor-causing bacteria, fungi, and mold spores.

_____ 13. Fiber ends are pulled from low-twist, spun yarns to create a soft, fuzzy surface on the fabric.

_____ 14. Chemicals that repel moths are added to dye baths to slightly change wool fibers.

_____ 15. Prevents static electricity and prevents garments from clinging to the wearer.

_____ 16. Finish added to tightly woven fabrics helps them resist water.

_____ 17. High temperatures are used to heat set fabrics or garments, which permanently creates the desired shapes, creases, and pleats.

_____ 18. The application of a metallic chemical to fabrics that include shower curtains and outdoor furniture.

A. antibacterial and antimicrobial
B. antistatic
C. calendering
D. crease-resistant and wrinkle-resistant
E. durable press and permanent press
F. fade-resistant
G. flame-resistant and flame-retardant
H. mildew-resistant
I. mercerization
J. moth-repellent
K. napping
L. shrinkage control
M. sizing
N. soil-release
O. stain-resistant
P. stone washing and acid wash
Q. water-repellent
R. weighting

Chapter 22 Figure Types and Pattern Sizes

Figure Types

Activity A Name _____

Chapter 22 Date _____ Period _____

Match the following figure types with their descriptions. Write the letter of the correct answer in the space provided.

_____ 1. Height 5'5" to 5'6". Average bust position. Average waist length. Fully-developed, well-proportioned figure considered to be the "average" figure, also the tallest.

_____ 2. Height 5'2" to 5'3". Low bust position. Short waist length. Short, fully-developed figure with narrow shoulders. Bust is smaller in proportion to waist and hips. Sometimes called half-size.

_____ 3. Approximately 5'10". Adult male figure of average build with fully developed shoulders, hips, and neck.

_____ 4. Height 5'2" to 5'3". Average bust position. Short waist length. Fully-developed, but shorter than Misses' figure.

_____ 5. No defined bustline. Short waist length. For the growing girl who has not yet begun to mature.

_____ 6. Height 4' to 5'8". Boys who have not yet reached full stature. Shoulders and hips are not as developed as those of a man.

_____ 7. Height 5'5" to 5'6". Average bust position. Average waist length. Proportionately larger, more mature figure with slightly longer back waist length measurement due to fuller back.

_____ 8. Slightly developed bustline. Short waist length. Young, growing girls' figure, over the average weight for their age and height.

A. Girls'
B. Girls' Plus
C. Misses'
D. Miss Petite
E. Women's
F. Women's Petite
G. Boys'/Teen-Boys'
H. Men's

Patterns and Measuring Techniques

Activity B Name _____
Chapter 22 Date _____ Period _____

Read the following statements. If the statement is true, write *true* in the blank. If the statement is false, write *false* in the blank. Answer the questions that follow.

_____ 1. Figure types refer to age.

_____ 2. Your figure type is based on your height, proportions, and body type.

_____ 3. Some of the figure types have their own sections in pattern catalogs.

_____ 4. *Tall* and *Short* are common figure types.

_____ 5. All pattern companies use the same standard sizes.

_____ 6. Pattern sizes are determined by bust or chest, waist, and hip or seat measurements.

_____ 7. Body measurements should be taken over bulky garments.

_____ 8. When taking measurements, the tape measure should be snug but not tight.

_____ 9. When taking a bust measurement, measure across the fullest part of the bust and straight across the back at the tips of the shoulder blades.

_____ 10. When taking a waist measurement, tie a string around the waist so the string will fall at your natural waistline.

_____ 11. When measuring the hips or seat, measure around the fullest part of the hips or seat.

_____ 12. Without ease, garments would be too tight, uncomfortable, and unattractive.

_____ 13. The waist needs more wearing ease than the hips.

_____ 14. Patterns designed for knitted fabrics only have less ease allowance than other patterns.

Why is it important to select the correct figure type and pattern size? _____
_____
_____
_____
_____

Why is it important to take accurate body measurements? _____
_____
_____
_____

Your Measurements

Activity C   **Name** _____

Chapter 22   **Date** _____   **Period** _____

Read the sections in the text about taking body measurements. In the chart that follows, write the measurements you need to take. With a classmate or family member, measure each other. Record your measurements in the chart. Then, using the information in the text, determine your figure type and pattern size and list it in the space provided after the chart.

Measurements to Take	Your Measurements	Pattern Body Measurements	Adjustments	
			+	−

My figure type is _____

My pattern size is _____

Chapter 22   Figure Types and Pattern Sizes

Selecting a Pattern

Activity D   Name _____

Chapter 22   Date _____ Period _____

Choose the body measurement that is most important when selecting a pattern for the various types of garments in the following list. Explain why this measurement is important for each garment.

    Chest measurement   Waist measurement
    Bust measurement   Hip measurement
    Shirt neck measurement

1. Blouse: _____
_____
_____

2. Dress: _____
_____
_____

3. Young woman's jacket: _____
_____
_____

4. Skirt: _____
_____
_____

5. Young woman's slacks and shorts: _____
_____
_____

6. Young man's shirt: _____
_____
_____

7. Men's sport coat: _____
_____
_____

8. Young men's vest: _____
_____
_____

9. Men's slacks and shorts: _____

Chapter 23
Selecting Patterns and Fabrics

Patterns and Projects

Activity A   **Name** _____

Chapter 23   **Date** _____ **Period** _____

Answer the following questions about pattern catalogs and patterns. Write your answers in the space provided.

1. Where can you look at patterns? _____
   _____

2. How is a pattern like a blueprint? _____
   _____

3. Why should you study the pattern in the pattern book until you are certain it is the one you want before you buy it? _____
   _____

4. What are the three main parts of a pattern? _____
   _____

5. What information can you find on the front of a pattern envelope? _____
   _____

6. What is the purpose of the cutting and sewing guide sheet? _____
   _____
   _____

7. In addition to patterns for garments, patterns are available for other types of projects. List four other items you could sew. _____
   _____
   _____

8. Give two examples of home décor items that could be made to decorate your living space.
   _____
   _____

Copyright Goodheart-Willcox Co., Inc. May not be reproduced or posted to a publicly accessible website.

Reading a Pattern Envelope

Activity B   Name _____

Chapter 23   Date _____ Period _____

Look at the sample pattern envelope back that follows. In the space provided, write the name of each item indicated by the numbers on the diagram.

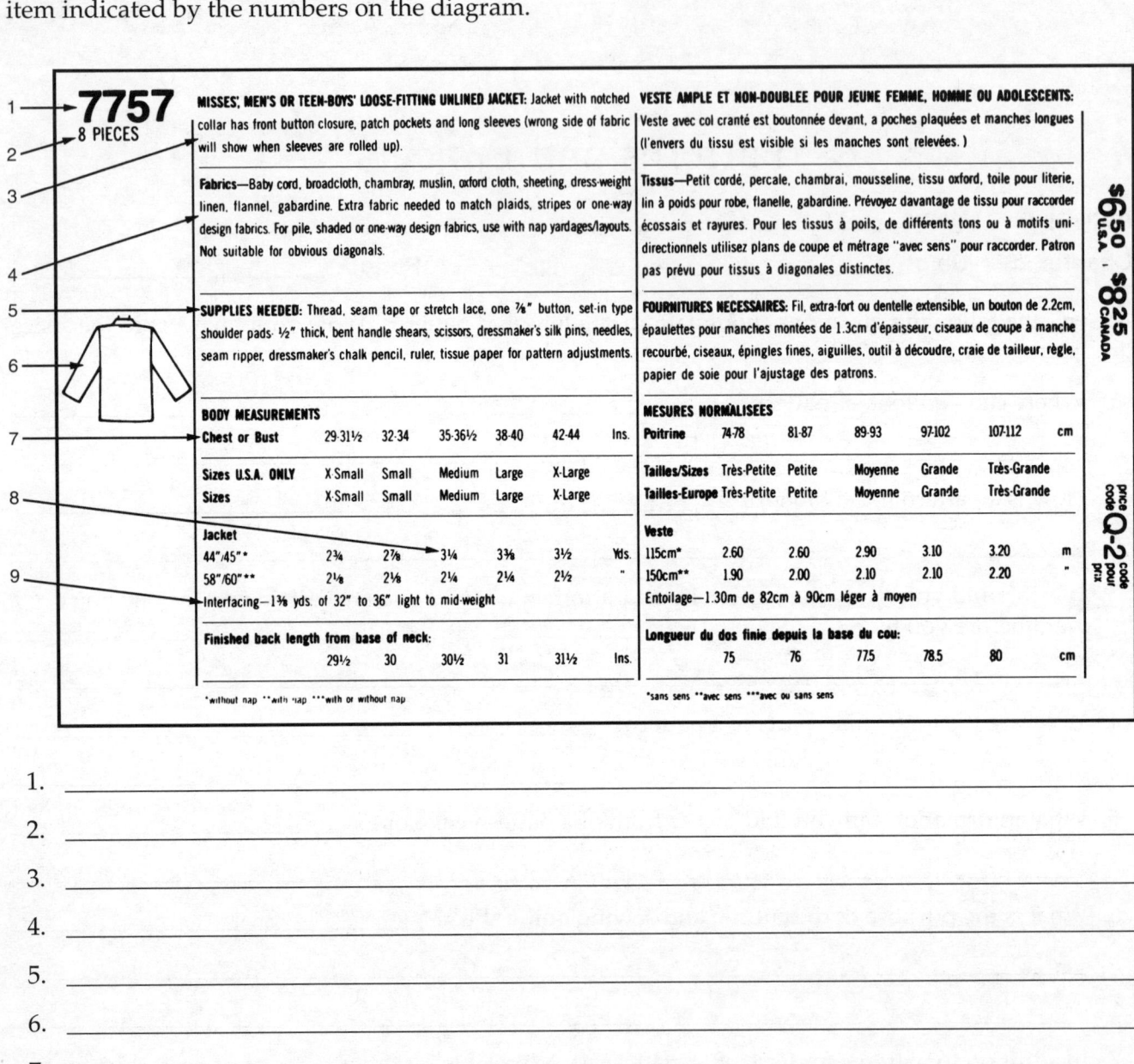

1. _____
2. _____
3. _____
4. _____
5. _____
6. _____
7. _____
8. _____
9. _____

Pattern Symbols

Activity C   Name _____

Chapter 23   Date _____   Period _____

Identify the pattern symbols indicated by the numbers on the pattern piece that follows. Write your answers in the space provided to the right of the corresponding numbers. Then briefly describe the purpose of each symbol in your own words.

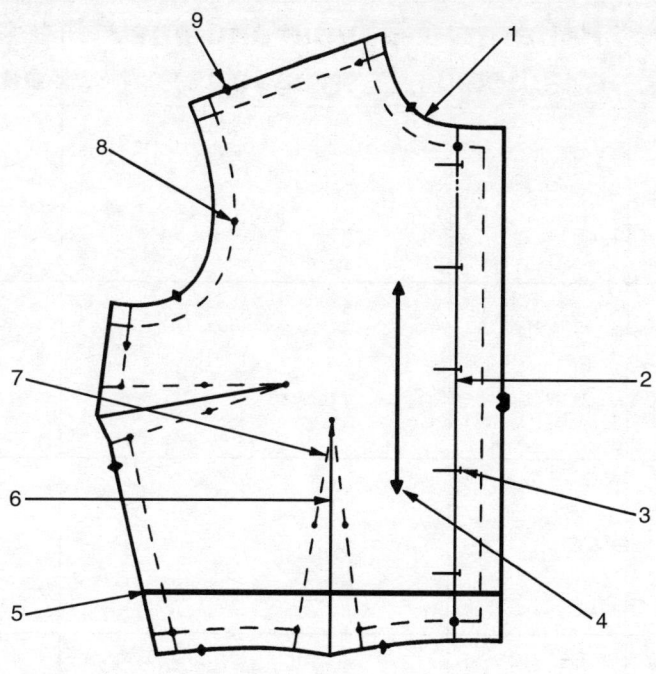

1. _____ : _____
2. _____ : _____
3. _____ : _____
4. _____ : _____
5. _____ : _____
6. _____ : _____
7. _____ : _____
8. _____ : _____
9. _____ : _____

Chapter 23   Selecting Patterns and Fabrics

Choosing the Right Pattern Designs

Activity D Name _____

Chapter 23 Date _____ Period _____

Look through print or online pattern catalogs. In the chart that follows, list six patterns that appeal to you. Decide whether the pattern would be simple and easy or advanced and difficult and give reasons for each. Then answer the following questions.

Pattern catalog (pattern company)	Pattern number	Simple and easy (reasons)	Difficult and advanced (reasons)
1.			
2.			
3.			
4.			
5.			
6.			

1. Which pattern would match your skill level? Explain. _____
   _____

2. Which pattern would fill a need in your wardrobe? Explain. _____
   _____

3. Which pattern design would flatter your body shape? Explain. _____
   _____

Chapter 24

Sewing Equipment

Equipment Uses

Activity A Name _____

Chapter 24 Date _____ Period _____

The diagrams that follow show some of the equipment you will need for sewing. Identify each piece of equipment and, in your own words, briefly describe how to use the equipment in the space provided.

1. _____
_____
_____

2. _____
_____
_____

3. _____
_____
_____

4. _____
_____
_____

5. _____
_____
_____

6. _____
_____
_____

(Continued)

133

Activity A, continued   Name_____

7. _____

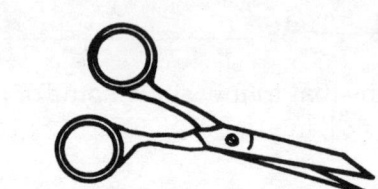

8. _____

9. _____

10. _____

11. _____

12. _____

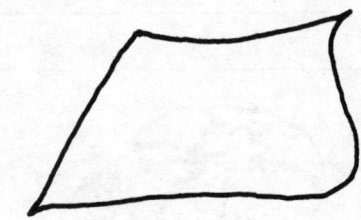

13. _____

14. _____

Notions

Activity B   Name _____

Chapter 24   Date _____   Period _____

Presume you are buying notions for a garment you plan to make. Answer the following questions. Write your responses in the space provided.

1. How do you find out what notions you will need for the garment? _____
   _____

_____ 2. When should you buy notions?
        A. As you need them.
        B. At the same time you buy your fabric.
        C. Ahead of time, when there is a sale.

_____ 3. If you are using a solid colored fabric, try to select thread that is _____.
        A. lighter in color than the fabric
        B. the exact same color as the fabric
        C. slightly darker than the fabric

_____ 4. If the fabric you are using is a polyester/cotton knit, which thread would be the best choice?
        A. Mercerized cotton thread.
        B. Polyester/cotton thread.
        C. Silk thread.

5. Name five types of fasteners you could use to close openings on garments. _____
   _____
   _____
   _____
   _____
   _____

6. True or false? Tapes and trims can be functional as well as decorative. _____

_____ 7. If you plan to stitch elastic directly to a garment, choose _____.
        A. woven elastic
        B. braided elastic
        C. elastic thread

_____ 8. When buying interfacing, choose interfacing _____.
        A. the same weight or a little lighter weight than your fabric
        B. heavier than the weight of your fabric
        C. that has the same care instructions as the other fabric you are using
        D. Both A and C.

Sewing Machine—Part Identification

Activity C Name _____

Chapter 24 Date _____ Period _____

Identify the various parts of the sewing machine. Write your responses in the space provided next to the corresponding numbers. On the following page, in your own words, briefly explain the purpose of each part in the space provided.

BERNINA International/BERNINA of America, Inc.

1. _____   5. _____

2. _____   6. _____

3. _____   7. _____

4. _____   8. _____

(Continued)

136 *Apparel: Design, Textiles & Construction* Workbook

Activity C, continued   Name _____

9. _____   17. _____
10. _____   18. _____
11. _____   19. _____
12. _____   20. _____
13. _____   21. _____
14. _____   22. _____
15. _____   23. _____
16. _____

1. _____
2. _____
3. _____
4. _____
5. _____
6. _____
7. _____
8. _____
9. _____
10. _____
11. _____
12. _____
13. _____
14. _____
15. _____
16. _____
17. _____
18. _____
19. _____
20. _____
21. _____
22. _____
23. _____

Sewing Machine Problem Detective

Activity D Name _____

Chapter 24 Date _____ Period _____

Sometimes you can solve sewing machine problems yourself. Presume you are a sewing machine detective. List the causes and cures of the various problems in the chart that follows.

Problem	Cause	Cure
1. Loud noise as you start to sew and matted threads in seamline.		
2. Lower thread breaks.		
3. Puckered seam line.		
4. Machine locks; needle will not go up and down.		
5. Skipped stitches.		
6. Looped stitches; top line; bottom line.		
7. Needle picks or pulls thread in line of stitching.		
8. Needle breaks.		
9. Machine runs "hard."		
10. Machine will not run at all.		

Chapter 25

Getting Ready to Sew

Fabric Grain

Activity A Name _____

Chapter 25 Date _____ Period _____

Identify the items related to fabric grain indicated by the numbers that follow. Write the correct term in the space provided to the right of the number. Then respond to the statement that follows.

1. _____
2. _____
3. _____
4. _____

Explain what would happen if you made a garment with a fabric that was off-grain. _____
_____
_____
_____
_____

Altering the Pattern

Activity B **Name** _____

Chapter 25 **Date** _____ **Period** _____

Under the diagrams that follow, indicate what actions have been taken to alter each of the pattern pieces. Write your responses in the space provided after each number.

1. _____
_____
_____
_____

2. _____
_____
_____
_____

3. _____
_____
_____
_____

4. _____
_____
_____
_____

140   *Apparel: Design, Textiles & Construction*   Workbook

Cutting Layouts

Activity C   Name _____

Chapter 25   Date _____   Period _____

Respond to the following statements and questions about this pattern guide sheet. Write your responses in the space provided.

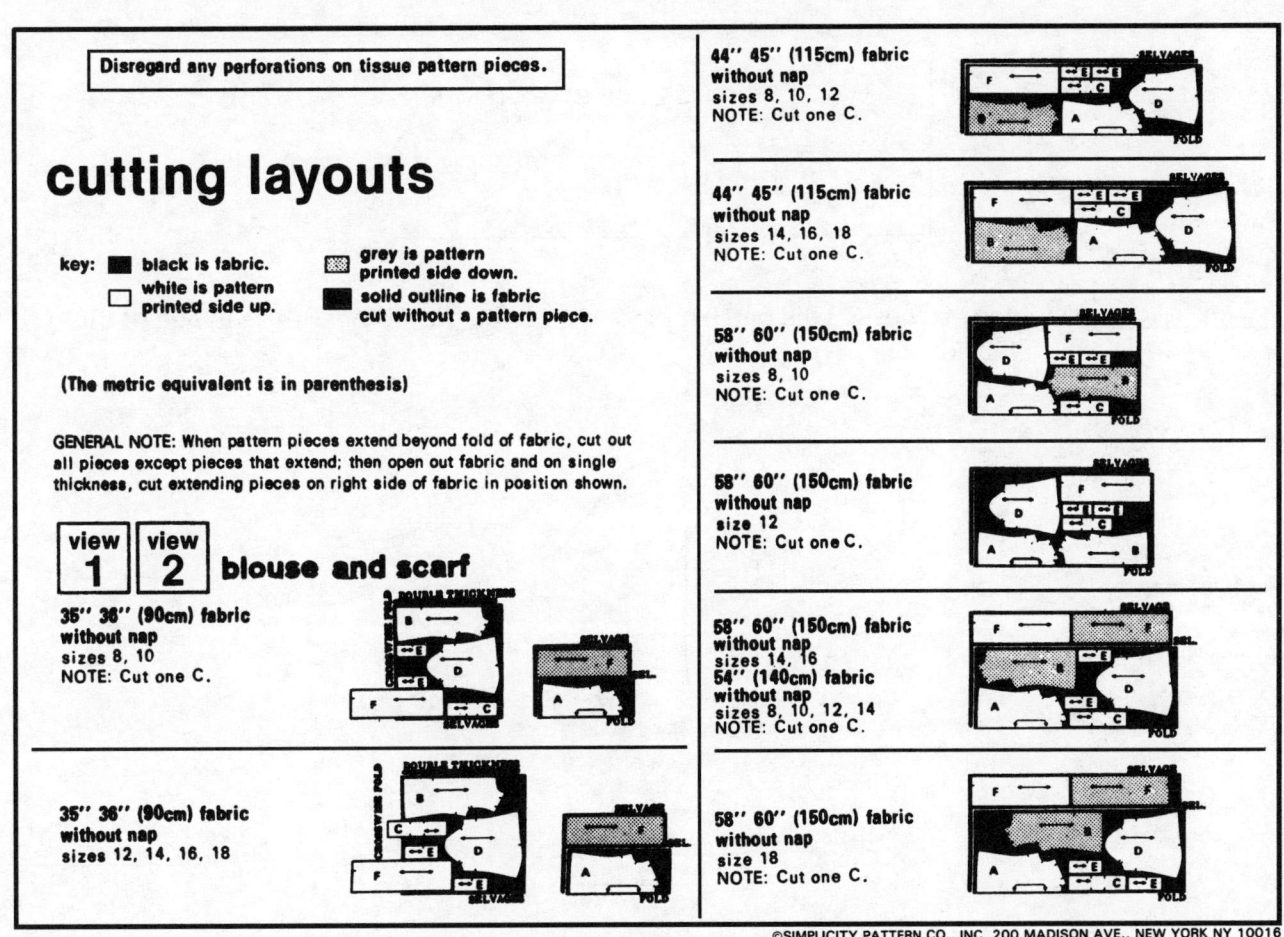

1. Suppose you are making the size 10 blouse and scarf and your fabric measures 44"–45" (115 cm). Which of the layouts above would use? _____

   _____

2. In the layout you have chosen, which pattern piece(s) would you place on the fabric with the printed side up? _____

   _____

3. In the layout you have chosen, which pattern piece(s) would you place on the fabric with the printed side down? _____

   _____

Pinning the Pattern Pieces

Activity D   Name _____

Chapter 25   Date _____ Period _____

Look at the diagrams that follow and respond to the statements. Record your responses in the space provided.

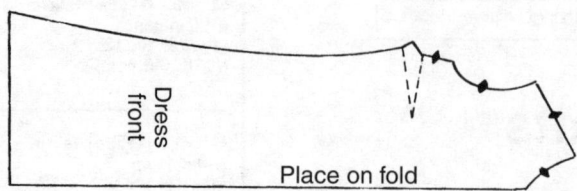

_____ 1. True or false? This pattern piece should be placed near the selvage of the fabric.

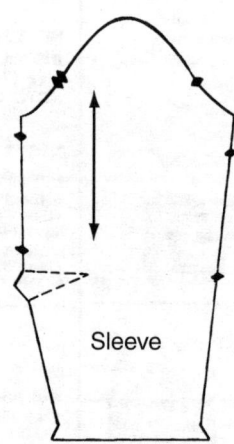

_____ 2. A straight line with arrows represents the _____ grain line.

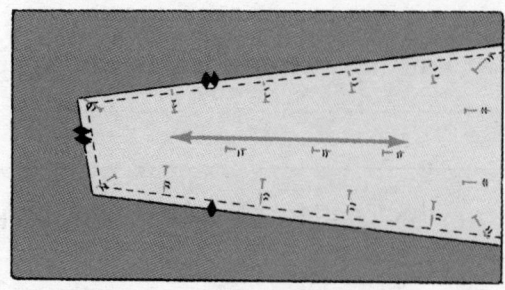

_____ 3. True or false? Are the pins on this pattern piece placed correctly?

Chapter 26

Basic Sewing Skills

Directional Sewing

Activity A   Name _____

Chapter 26   Date _____ Period _____

Look at the pattern pieces and arrows indicating directional sewing. If the arrows are correct, write *correct* in the blank provided with each drawing. If the arrows are incorrect, write *incorrect* in the blank.

1. _____ _____

2. _____ _____

3. _____ _____

4. _____ _____

5. _____ _____

6. _____ _____

143

Copyright Goodheart-Willcox Co., Inc. May not be reproduced or posted to a publicly accessible website.

Seams and Seam Finishes

Activity B   **Name** _____

Chapter 26   **Date** _____   **Period** _____

Identify the following seams and seam finishes. Briefly explain when to use each. Record your responses in the space provided. Then, use 4-inch by 4-inch fabric swatches to make samples similar to these. Present your samples to the rest of the class.

1. _____
   _____
   _____
   _____

2. _____
   _____
   _____
   _____

3. _____
   _____
   _____
   _____

4. _____
   _____
   _____
   _____

(Continued)

Activity B, continued   Name _____

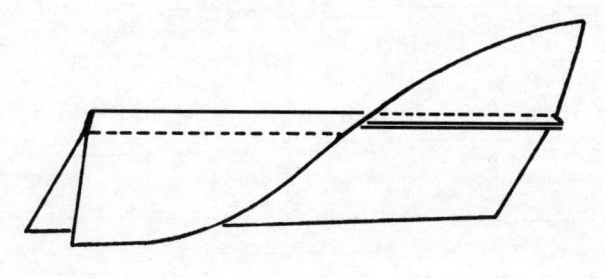

5. _____

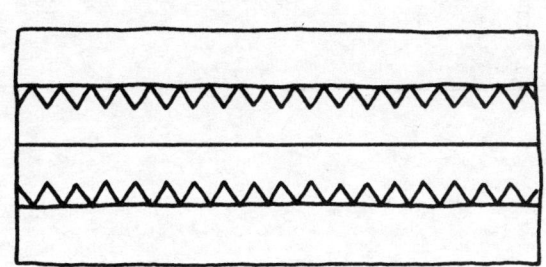

6. _____

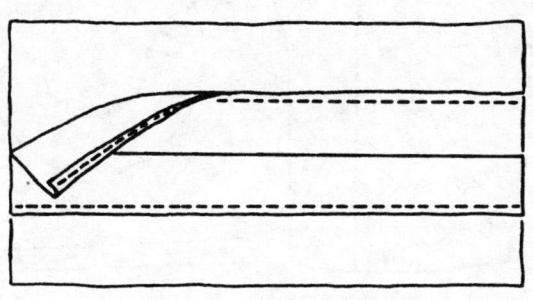

7. _____

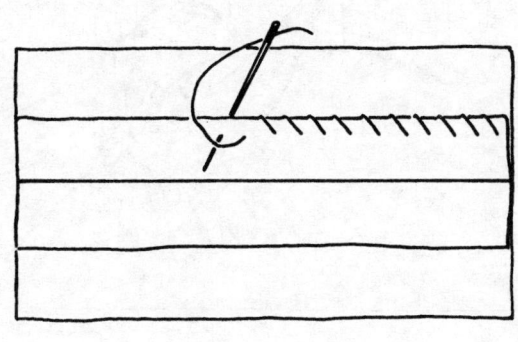

8. _____

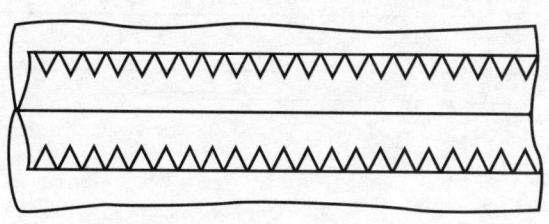

9. _____

10. _____

Facings and Interfacings

Activity C   **Name** _____

Chapter 26   **Date** _____   **Period** _____

Complete the following exercise on facings and interfacings. Write your answers in the space provided.

1. Explain why facings are used. _____
   _____

2. Where are facings used? _____
   _____

3. Identify the three types of facings.

   A. _____

   B. _____

   C. _____

4. _____ is a row of stitches placed close to the seam line through the facing and seam allowances to prevent the facing from rolling to the outside.

5. Identify the items indicated on the illustration below.

   A. _____

   B. _____

   C. _____

   D. _____

6. What is the purpose of interfacing? _____
   _____

7. Where is interfacing used? _____
   _____

8. Name three types of interfacing. _____
   _____
   _____

Hem Finishes and Hems

Activity D Name _____

Chapter 26 Date _____ Period _____

Identify the following hem finishes and hems. In the space provided, briefly explain when you would use each. Use 4-inch by 4-inch fabric swatches to make samples similar to these. Present your samples to the rest of the class.

1. _____
_____
_____
_____

2. _____
_____
_____
_____

3. _____
_____
_____
_____

4. _____
_____
_____
_____

(Continued)

Chapter 26 Basic Sewing Skills

Activity D, continued Name _____

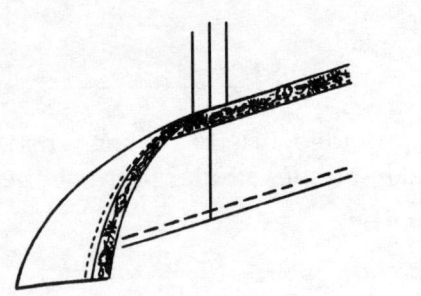

5. _____

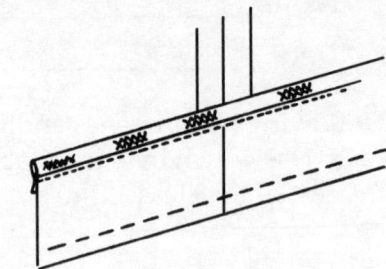

6. _____

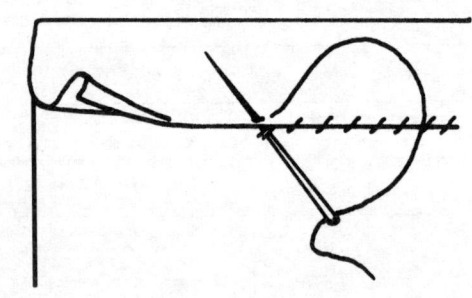

7. _____

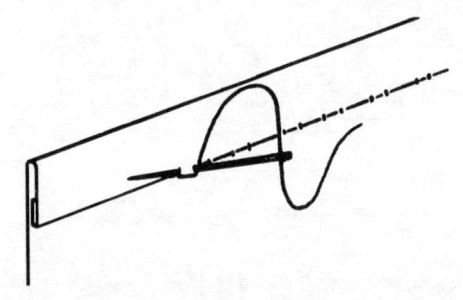

8. _____

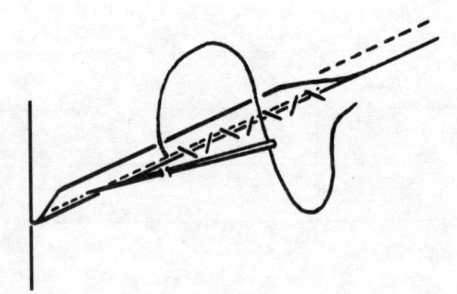

9. _____

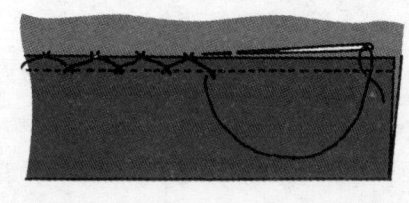

10. _____

Chapter 27

Advanced Sewing Skills

Collars

Activity A Name _____

Chapter 27 Date _____ Period _____

Complete the following exercise about collars. Write your responses in the space provided.

1. Identify the three basic styles of collars and describe them as follows.

    A. _____
    _____
    _____

    B. _____
    _____
    _____

    C. _____
    _____
    _____

2. Collars need the support provided by _____.

3. After stitching a collar using a full-fitted facing, in which order should you do the following steps?
    _____ Grade
    _____ Clip
    _____ Trim
    _____ Understitch

_____ 4. True or false? A standing collar is usually attached with no facing.

Sleeves

Activity B   Name _____

Chapter 27   Date _____   Period _____

Complete the following exercise on sleeves. Write your responses in the space provided.

    A   B   C

1. Identify the three basic styles of sleeves and describe them below.

    A. _____
        _____
        _____

    B. _____
        _____
        _____

    C. _____
        _____
        _____

2. Look through magazines or use Internet sources to find a picture of a blouse or shirt that has sleeves. Paste a copy of the image or URL address in the space provided. Identify the type of sleeve and describe how it was most likely constructed.

Sleeve type: _____

150   *Apparel: Design, Textiles & Construction*   Workbook

Pockets

Activity C   **Name** _____

Chapter 27   **Date** _____ **Period** _____

Complete the following exercise on pockets. Write your responses in the space provided.

1. Identify the types of pockets as shown and describe how they are constructed.

A.

A. _____
_____
_____
_____
_____

B.

B. _____
_____
_____
_____
_____

C.

C. _____
_____
_____
_____
_____

2. Name the type of pocket you would most likely find on the following garments.

Garment	Type of Pocket
A. Shirt (front):	_____
B. Shorts (side):	_____
C. Skirt (front):	_____
D. Jeans (front):	_____
E. Skirt (side):	_____

Chapter 27   Advanced Sewing Skills

Sewing with Knits and Pile Fabrics

Activity D Name _____

Chapter 27 Date _____ Period _____

Look through magazines or use Internet sources to find images of fabric samples of four types of knit and/or pile fabrics. Paste a copy of the images or URL addresses in the spaces provided. Find out any special considerations you would need to make for sewing with each of these fabrics and list them in the space provided.

Fabric:
Special considerations:

_____

_____

_____

Fabric:
Special considerations:

_____

_____

_____

Fabric:
Special considerations:

_____

_____

_____

Fabric:
Special considerations:

_____

_____

_____

Chapter 28 — Serging Skills

Sergers

Activity A   Name _____

Chapter 28   Date _____   Period _____

Complete the following activity about sewing with a serger. Write your responses in the space provided.

1. Identify the process taking place in the illustration above. _____
   _____

2. Describe what a serger does. _____
   _____

3. Explain why a serger supplements a conventional sewing machine but does not replace it. _____
   _____
   _____

4. What types of fabrics can you sew with a serger? _____
   _____

5. A serger can give a professional seam _____ to garments such as unlined jackets.

6. Some _____ can stitch at a speed of 1300 to 1500 stitches per minute. The average top speed of a _____ sewing machine is 900 to 1000 stitches per minute.

7. Have you ever used a serger? If so, give examples of projects you have made using a serger. ____
   _____
   _____

Serger Machine Parts

Activity B Name _____

Chapter 28 Date _____ Period _____

Identify the various major parts of the serger and the parts inside the serger cover on the following page. Write your responses in the space provided.

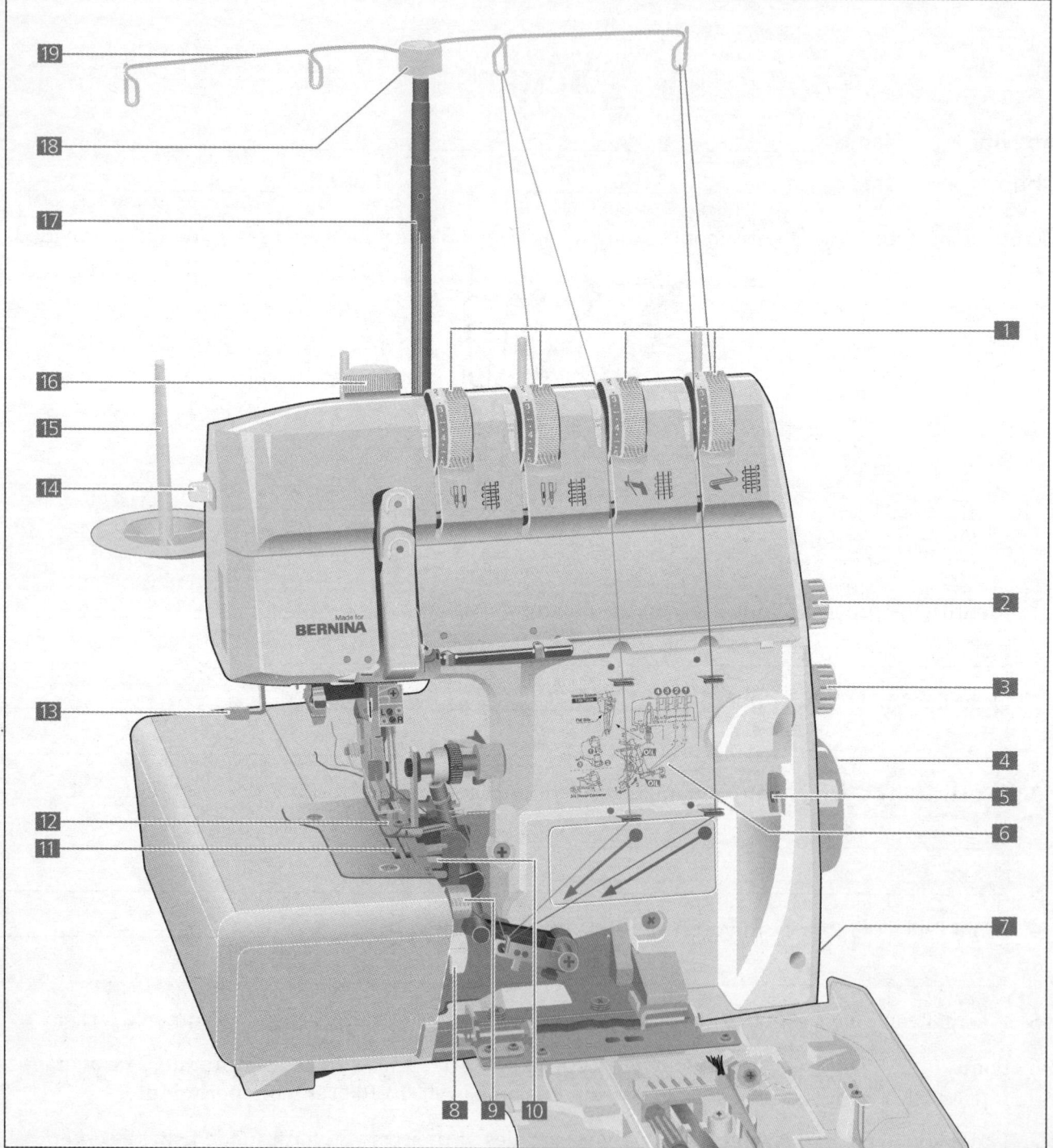

Photo courtesy of BERNINA International/BERNINA of America, Inc.

(Continued)

Activity B, continued   Name_____

1. _____
2. _____
3. _____
4. _____
5. _____
6. _____
7. _____
8. _____
9. _____
10. _____

11. _____
12. _____
13. _____
14. _____
15. _____
16. _____
17. _____
18. _____
19. _____

Image courtesy of BERNINA International/BERNINA of America, Inc.

1. _____
2. _____
3. _____
4. _____
5. _____
6. _____
7. _____
8. _____
9. _____

Serger Stitch Identification

Activity C   **Name** _____

Chapter 28   **Date** _____   **Period** _____

Identify the serger stitches shown and describe when they would be used. Write your responses in the space provided.

1. _____
_____
_____

2. _____
_____
_____

3. _____
_____
_____

4. _____
_____
_____

5. _____
_____
_____

6. _____
_____
_____

Photos courtesy of BERNINA International/BERNINA of America, Inc.

Parts of Serger Stitches

Activity D   **Name** _____

Chapter 28   **Date** _____ **Period** _____

Identify the various parts of the serger stitches as shown in the following. Write your responses in the space provided.

1. _____
2. _____
3. _____
4. _____
5. _____
6. _____
7. _____

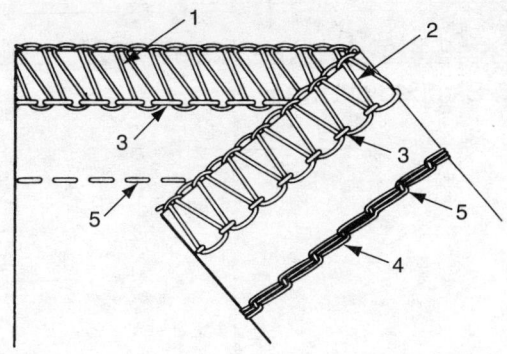

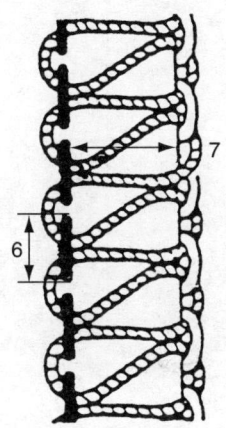

Chapter 28   Serging Skills   157

Serger Problems and Solutions

Activity E   **Name** _____

Chapter 28   **Date** _____   **Period** _____

Sometimes you can solve serger problems yourself. Look at the following chart. Determine the possible solution to each of the problems listed. Write your solutions in the space provided.

Problem	Possible Solutions
1. Skipped stitches	
2. Thread breaks	
3. Fabric jams	
4. Needle breaks	
5. Fabric puckers	

Chapter 29

Preparing for a Career

Leadership Skills and Traits

Activity A   Name _____

Chapter 29   Date _____ Period _____

Review the following list of various leadership skills and traits. If a skill or trait is a *positive* one, write P in the blank. If the skill or trait is a *negative* one, write N in the blank.

_____ 1. Does all the work and will not allow others to do tasks.

_____ 2. Keeps an open mind about decisions and situations and is willing to listen to new ideas.

_____ 3. Is not confident in making a decision.

_____ 4. Is able to delegate responsibilities to those best qualified.

_____ 5. Is flexible, can accept change, and can help others accept change, too.

_____ 6. Does not consider the alternatives and consequences when dealing with a problem.

_____ 7. Has the confidence to make a decision and carry it out.

_____ 8. Is inflexible and does not accept change.

_____ 9. Is good at problem-solving.

_____ 10. Is closed-minded about decisions and situations, and is not willing to listen to new ideas.

_____ 11. Feels that communication is unnecessary.

_____ 12. Is self-confident and shows a strong sense of responsibility.

_____ 13. Is enthusiastic and can motivate others to do their best.

_____ 14. Stresses cooperation and sets a good example.

_____ 15. Supervises work, but does not participate in getting the job done.

_____ 16. Lacks confidence.

_____ 17. Has good communication skills and can express thoughts clearly and effectively.

_____ 18. Helps the team reach its goals.

_____ 19. Is shy.

_____ 20. Makes it difficult for the team to reach its goals.

List one of the leadership skills or traits you would like to develop. _____

How would this leadership skill or trait help you in a student organization and in a future career?

_____

_____

159

Copyright Goodheart-Willcox Co., Inc. May not be reproduced or posted to a publicly accessible website.

Effective Working Relationships

Activity B   **Name** _____

Chapter 29   **Date** _____ **Period** _____

Give examples of situations in which interpersonal and communication skills can help you in organizations you belong to now, and help you to be a better employee in the future. Write your responses in the space provided. Compare and discuss your responses with those of class members.

1. Having empathy. _____
   _____

2. Showing respect for other people's feelings and needs. _____
   _____

3. Willingness to give and take when differences arise. _____
   _____

4. Being able to accept criticism without taking offense. _____
   _____

5. Having a sense of humor. _____
   _____

6. Keeping a positive attitude. _____
   _____

7. Being honest and trustworthy. _____
   _____

8. Showing dependability. _____
   _____

9. Having good speaking ability. _____
   _____

10. Being a good listener. _____
    _____

Student Organizations

Activity C   **Name** _____

Chapter 29   **Date** _____   **Period** _____

Complete the following chart about student organizations. Then visit a meeting for one of the student organizations on the list and answer the questions that follow the chart. Write your responses in the space provided.

Student Organization	Purpose
Family, Career and Community Leaders of America (FCCLA)	
National FFA Organization (FFA)	
DECA—An Association of Marketing Students	
Future Business Leaders of America (FBLA-PBL)	
Health Occupations Students of America (HOSA)	
Educators Rising	
SkillsUSA	

Name of student organization meeting you attended: _____

How does this organization provide opportunities for leadership and teamwork? _____

_____

_____

_____

_____

Why would you be interested in joining this organization? Explain your answer. _____

_____

_____

_____

_____

Chapter 29   Preparing for a Career

Parliamentary Procedure and Meetings

Activity D   Name _____

Chapter 29   Date _____   **Period** _____

Complete the following exercises about parliamentary procedure and organizational business meetings.

Unscramble the order of business outline in *Robert's Rules of Order* by numbering the following parts of a meeting (from 1 to 10) in the order described in the text. Write your responses in the space provided.

_____ Reports of the officers

_____ Unfinished business

_____ Standing committee reports

_____ Announcements

_____ Reading and approving of minutes

_____ Adjournment

_____ Special committee reports

_____ Call to order

_____ The program

_____ New business

The following terms are often used in meetings. Match each term in the right column with its description in the left column by writing the correct letter in the blank.

_____ 1. To end a meeting.

_____ 2. A list of things to do and discuss at a meeting.

_____ 3. To change the wording of a motion that has been made.

_____ 4. The presiding officer at a meeting, such as the president or chairperson.

_____ 5. To speak for or against a motion.

_____ 6. At least one more than half of the members present at a meeting.

_____ 7. A written record of the business covered at a meeting.

_____ 8. A suggestion by a member that a certain action be taken by the group.

_____ 9. The number of members who must be present to legally conduct business at a meeting.

_____ 10. The approval of a motion by another member.

_____ 11. To delay making a decision on a motion.

_____ 12. The right to speak in a meeting without interruption from others.

_____ 13. The motion on which members are called to vote.

A. table the question
B. motion
C. the question
D. chair
E. adjourn
F. majority
G. minutes
H. second the motion
I. the floor
J. quorum
K. debate
L. agenda
M. amend the motion

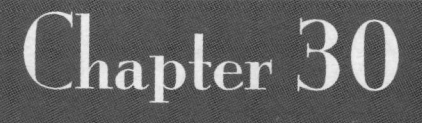

A Job and a Career

A Career in Textiles and Apparel

Activity A   **Name** _____

Chapter 30   **Date** _____ **Period** _____

Investigate a career of your choice in the textile and apparel field. Begin by surveying the 16 career clusters. If possible, interview someone with your career of interest. You may use library resources, information from your guidance counselor, and the Internet. Find out the following information and share it with the class. Write your responses in the space provided.

Career: _____

Career cluster: _____

Education or training needed: _____
_____

Salary range: _____

Description of duties: _____
_____

Hours: _____

Working conditions: _____
_____

Advantages of this career: _____
_____
_____

Disadvantages of this career: _____
_____
_____

Other comments: _____
_____
_____

Self-Study

Activity B Name _____

Chapter 30 Date _____ Period _____

Doing a self-study and exploring the career clusters helps enable you to choose a career that is right for you. Look at the interest statements below. Place a check on the scale to indicate your level of interest in each of the following. (There are no right or wrong answers.)

Yes	Maybe	No	
____	____	____	1. I like to work by myself.
____	____	____	2. I like to work with other people.
____	____	____	3. I am a good organizer.
____	____	____	4. I like a challenge.
____	____	____	5. I like to express my creativity.
____	____	____	6. I like to make decisions.
____	____	____	7. I would prefer to travel a great deal.
____	____	____	8. I would like a desk job.
____	____	____	9. I want to use design skills.
____	____	____	10. I want to use math skills.
____	____	____	11. I want to do research.
____	____	____	12. I like to follow directions.
____	____	____	13. I want to work with tools and machines.
____	____	____	14. I like working with the public.
____	____	____	15. I like repetitious work.
____	____	____	16. I like work that is continuously changing.
____	____	____	17. I like working under pressure.
____	____	____	18. I work best in a calm, relaxed atmosphere.
____	____	____	19. I like to work long hours.
____	____	____	20. Others:

Based on your responses above, list a career you feel would be right for you. Explain why this career would be a good choice for you.

_____
_____
_____

How can knowing your likes and dislikes help you in choosing the right career for you?

_____
_____
_____

Preparing a Résumé

Activity C **Name** _____

Chapter 30 **Date** _____ **Period** _____

Design a résumé for yourself in the space provided. Decide whether you need a *chronological* or *functional* résumé. (Refer to the sample résumés in Figure 30-7A and B of the text.) Read your résumé carefully. Ask your teacher or counselor to read it, too. When you are happy with your résumé, use a computer with word-processing software to create a final copy. Print your résumé on good-quality paper. (You may wish to make copies of your résumé to submit to potential employers.)

A Cover Message

Activity D Name _____

Chapter 30 Date _____ Period _____

Think about a job you would like to have and then research openings for that job in print or online sources. In the following space, write a cover message for the job. (Refer to Figure 30-8 in the text for a sample cover message.)

Filling out a Job Application Form

Activity E   **Name** _____

Chapter 30   **Date** _____   **Period** _____

Complete the following sample job application form. Use black or blue ink, write neatly, and complete all applicable information in the space provided.

APPLICATION FOR EMPLOYMENT

PERSONAL INFORMATION

Date _____

Name _____
      Last   First   Middle

Present Address _____
      Street   City   State

Permanent Address _____
      Street   City   State

Phone No. _____

If related to anyone in our employ, state name and department. _____   Referred by _____

EMPLOYMENT DESIRED

Position _____   Date you can start _____   Salary desired _____

Are you employed now? _____   If so, may we inquire of your present employer? _____

Ever applied to this company before? _____   Where? _____   When? _____

EDUCATION

	Name and Location of School	Years Completed	Subjects Studied
Grammar School			
High School			
College			
Trade, Business, or Correspondence School			

Subject of special study or research work _____

What foreign languages do you speak fluently? _____   Read? _____   Write? _____

(Continued)

Activity E, continued Name_____

| U.S. Military or Naval service | Rank | Present membership in National Guard or Reserves |

Activities other than religious, civic, athletic, fraternal, etc. Exclude organizations in which the name or character indicates the race, creed, color, or national origin of its members.

_____

FORMER EMPLOYERS List below last three employers starting with last one first.

Date Month and Year	Name and Address of Employer	Salary	Position	Reason for Leaving
From				
To				
From				
To				
From				
To				

REFERENCES Give below the names of two persons not related to you, whom you have known for at least one year.

	Name	Address	Job Title	Years Acquainted
1				
2				

PHYSICAL RECORD

Have you any disabilities that might affect your job performance?

_____

In case of emergency notify

| | Name | Address | Phone No. |

I authorize investigation of all statements contained in this application. I understand that misrepresentation or omission of facts called for is cause for dismissal.

Date_____ Signature_____

The Job Interview

Activity F Name _____

Chapter 30 Date _____ Period _____

Questions that are often asked during a job interview are listed below. Presume you are being interviewed. Answer these questions as you would during an interview.

Job for which you are applying: _____

Company: _____

1. Why do you want to work for this company? What attracted you to this job? _____
   _____
   _____

2. Do you think you will like this kind of work? _____ Why? _____
   _____
   _____

3. How would you describe yourself? _____
   _____
   _____

4. What are your best subjects in school? _____
   _____

5. What are your worst subjects in school? _____
   _____

6. What other jobs have you had? _____
   _____
   _____

7. What accomplishments have you had that show your ability to handle this type of work? _____
   _____
   _____
   _____

8. What is your major weakness? _____
   _____

9. What are your career goals? _____
   _____

10. Why should we hire you? _____
    _____
    _____

Using Time Wisely

Activity G   Name _____

Chapter 30   Date _____   Period _____

An important part of personal and workplace success is how well you use your time, both at home and at work. Keep track of your time for a week. Record your activities in the space provided and indicate how much time you will need to accomplish each task. Then, respond to the following questions.

Weekly Activities	Time Needed for Task

1. How well did you manage your time throughout the week? _____
   _____
   _____
   _____
   _____

2. Which time-management techniques would you like to develop? _____
   _____
   _____
   _____
   _____

Chapter 31
Entrepreneurship—Profiting from Your Skills

Entrepreneur Interview

Activity A   **Name** _____

Chapter 31   **Date** _____   **Period** _____

Interview a local entrepreneur. Find out the following information and write it in the space provided. With permission from the entrepreneur, use the responses to write an article about him or her on the following page. Submit the article to your school newspaper or a local newspaper.

Name of entrepreneur: _____

Name of business: _____

Location of business: _____

Describe the business: _____
_____
_____

What made you decide to start this business? _____
_____
_____
_____

What personal characteristics help you succeed in this business? _____
_____
_____
_____

What are the pros of being an entrepreneur? _____
_____
_____
_____

(Continued)

Activity A, continued   Name_____

What are the cons of being an entrepreneur?_____
_____
_____
_____

What advice would you give to someone considering becoming an entrepreneur? _____
_____
_____
_____
_____

Additional comments:
_____
_____
_____
_____
_____
_____
_____
_____

Entrepreneur Article

_____
_____
_____
_____
_____
_____
_____
_____

Profiting from Your Skills

Activity B   **Name** _____

Chapter 31   **Date** _____   **Period** _____

Look through pattern books and magazines and visit some craft shows and craft stores to obtain ideas about items you might like to make to sell. Then complete the following exercise. Write your responses in the space provided.

1. List items you would like to make to sell. _____
   _____
   _____
   _____

2. Which item above would your customers most likely buy? _____
   _____

3. Describe the item. _____
   _____
   _____

4. List the materials and cost of materials below.

Materials	Cost
_____	_____
_____	_____
_____	_____
_____	_____
_____	_____
_____	_____
	Total $ _____

5. How much time would it take you to produce and sell the item? _____

6. How much do you want to earn per hour? _____

7. Multiply the amount in #6 by the number of hours in #5. _____

8. How much profit do you want to make? _____

9. Add the totals from #4, #7, and #8 to arrive at the approximate price of the item. _____

10. Where would you sell your items? _____
    _____
    _____
    _____

Entrepreneurship

Activity C   Name _____

Chapter 31   Date _____ Period _____

Complete the following activity about entrepreneurship. Write your responses in the space provided.

1. What does becoming an entrepreneur mean to you? _____
   _____

2. Does starting your own business appeal to you? _____ Give two reasons for your answer.
   _____
   _____

3. List at least three products or services you could sell. _____
   _____
   _____
   _____

4. Briefly describe the demand for your products or services. (Consider potential customers, competition, and your abilities.) _____
   _____
   _____
   _____

5. Based on your answer in #4, which product or service seems to offer you the best opportunity for success? _____

6. How much time would your business take to manage? _____
   Do you have enough time to accomplish this? _____

7. How much money do you estimate it would cost to start and operate your business? (Consider factors such as equipment, supplies, and advertising.)
   _____
   _____

8. Consider your answers to the above questions. What are some advantages and disadvantages of becoming an entrepreneur?

   Advantages: _____
   _____
   _____

   Disadvantages: _____
   _____
   _____